Dedicated to

the memory of family members who have passed before me, especially Vera

My Life

Bernard Verosub

"My Story" Copyright © 2011 by Bernard Verosub.

    ISBN-13: 978-1-46350386-4.
    ISBN-10: 1463503865.

All rights reserved. No part of this publication may be reproduced, stored in a retrieval system, or transmitted in any form or by any means, electronic, mechanical, recording, or otherwise, without the prior permission of the author, Bernard Verosub.

Manufactured in the United States of America.

Acknowledgments

My Life has been fifteen years in the making, but the project was finally completed with the help of others who I would like to acknowledge here:

Skylands RSVP & Volunteer Resource Center, in connection with Northwest NJ Community Action Program Inc. (NORWESCAP), links the skills of volunteers with local organizations. Ellen Konwiser, special projects coordinator for NORWESCAP, came up with the idea of the Lifebook Writing Project, which began several years ago in Morris County and which is now branching into Passaic County. Ellen felt that "nobody's life is boring," and she recruited volunteers to prove it. The volunteers work with seniors to record their life experiences for their families.

Sharon Palmer is the volunteer who was assigned to my story, and we collaborated almost weekly over a seven-month period, working on my story. As we've traveled this road together, we've found that we have similar interests and have developed a friendship.

Sharon recruited her husband, Rob, who has extensively traversed the world of book publication, and he proved invaluable in laying out the book, designing the cover, and handling the technical details of getting my story published.

Rob then called upon his brother, Steve, an expert in the world of photo editing, who was able to enhance and reconstruct the picture on the cover of this book. The picture features my grandfather, Reuben (on the right), and his two brothers, Vladimir and Aaron.

So, it was with the help of others that I completed my story and finished the project I had started so long ago. I thank them all, and I am grateful for their interest and help.

Author's Notes

I started *My Life*, the story of the Verozub (Verosub) and Golostupitz (Golos) families, about fifteen years ago, tapping out the details on my computer, adding to it periodically over the years. Although I tried a number of times to make an audio recording, it just didn't work out until recently when I received help from a volunteer who convinced me to try again. So talk I did, and record she did. Each week she transcribed my words and then I would review the week's work. This went on for about seven months. Of course, I could have included a lot more about family members and friends and my ninety-plus years of life, but you have to stop someplace.

I did it for the children, the grandchildren, and the great-grandchildren. I wanted them to know their family history and those who came before them, the good times and the bad, and I didn't want our ancestors to be forgotten.

At the age of 70, I had one story to tell. At the age of 80, I had ten stories to tell. But now that I'm past 90, the sky's the limit.

— Bernard Verosub

My Life

Bernard Verosub

My Life

My grandparents, Reuben and Nahama Verozub and Lieb and Esther Golostupitz, all resided in Kiev, in the Ukraine, which was part of Russia at the end of the 1800s. The Verozub siblings consisted of Nicolia (Kolia, my father), Elieser (Lazar or Leo), Gita, Lisa, Dvera, and Rosa. The Golostupitz siblings consisted of Fenta (Anuta, my mother), Octavius, Anatole, Misha, Hannah, Klara and Basia. Reuben Verozub had a business that would be similar to a salvage yard. Scavengers would bring all sorts of goods to the yard that he would buy and sell to various industries. Lieb Golostupitz was a carpenter and had a woodworking shop, but did not work on construction.

Some important dates: Nicolia (Kolia), born January 5, 1891; Anita (Anuta), born March 23, 1895; Octave (Octavius), born 1885; Morris (Misha), born November 1, 1891; and Leo (Elieser), born January 5, 1894.

In 1905, Russia was at war with Japan. Young men were being drafted into the army, and the term of conscription for Jewish men was twenty-five years. Octavius was of draft age, so he decided to leave Russia. He traveled by night across the Ukraine and Poland, hiding during the day, until he reached the German border, where he took a train to Paris, France. For about a year, he was able to get jobs to cover his living expenses. Toward the end of 1906, he obtained an apprenticeship as a designer and fitter of ladies' fur coats at the fashion salon of Don Loper.

My parents, Kolia and Anuta, were married on February 19, 1912, when they were 21 and 17 years of age. On the 9th of December, 1913, they left Russia and went to France to join Octavius in Paris, with Kolia's brother, Elieser, and Anuta's brother, Misha, traveling with them. When they arrived in Paris, they located Octavius and found a place to live. The four of them spoke only Russian, and so Kolia and Elieser were restricted to jobs as busboys in a restaurant. Anuta, being pregnant, did not look for employment. Misha had been an apprentice in a printing shop in Russia. When he heard there was a printing shop in need of men who were able to handset Russian type, he went there and was immediately hired. This shop was printing propaganda for the Russian Bolshevik[1] (Communist) Party. While working in the print shop, Misha met Vladimir Lenin[2] and Leon Trotsky[3].

In early 1914, Anuta gave birth to a baby girl. Four months later, the baby died from malnutrition. The war broke out, and all of Europe was involved. In September, the first Battle of the Marne began, and the German army advanced on Paris. There was a tremendous exodus from the city; many took taxicabs to leave Paris. The family of five went to Lyon where there was an International Exposition. All of them were now fluent in French, so were able to get jobs at the Exposition, Kolia and Anuta being assigned to The United States Pavilion. At the Exposition's closing in November, the family went to Marseille where, once again, the employment problem was acute.

Kolia and Elieser found jobs in restaurants, Anuta worked in a bakery and Misha found work in a print shop. They were

---

[1] The Bolsheviks, founded by Vladimir Lenin, were a faction of the Marxist Russian Social Democratic Labour Party, coming to power in Russia during the 1917 Russian Revolution and founding the Soviet Union. They ultimately became the Communist Party of the Soviet Union. The Bolsheviks considered themselves the leaders of the revolutionary working class of Russia. Their beliefs and practices were often referred to as Bolshevism.

[2] Vladimir Ilyich Lenin (1870 – 1924) was a Russian Marxist revolutionary, author, lawyer, political philosopher, creator of the Soviet Communist Party, leader of the 1917 October Revolution, and founder of the USSR. As head of the Bolsheviks (1917–1924), he led the Red Army to victory in the Russian Civil War before establishing the world's first officially socialist state.

[3] Leon Trotsky (1879 – 1940) was a Bolshevik revolutionary and Marxist theorist, second only to Vladimir Lenin. Trotsky founded the Red Army and was one of the organizers of the 1917 Russian October Revolution which eventually led to victory in the Russian Civil War and the 1922 establishment of the Soviet Union.

impressed with the pictures they had seen while working at the American pavilion and with the stories about life in America. The four of them decided to migrate to America, with Octavius eventually returning to Paris.

While living in Paris and Lyon, Kolia and Anuta had become friends with Abraham and Farina Lomaskin. It was decided that they would all go to Bordeaux, a port in the southwestern part of France, to arrange passage to America. Kolia, Misha, and Abraham were able to get passage, and they departed on July 4, 1915 aboard the steamship *Rochambeau*. They arrived at Ellis Island, New York, on July 13, 1915.

Kolia knew Abraham and Celia Lande who had three daughters and a son in New York. Abraham Lande had worked as the yard foreman for Reuben Verozub in Kiev. Kolia stayed with them until he was able to find an apartment, and when the rest of the family arrived in August, they all moved into the new apartment. Although Abraham and Celia Lande spoke Russian, Yiddish and a little English, neither of them could read or write any of these languages, nor could Abraham read Hebrew. This caused a problem for the Lande family when it came time for the Passover Seder, and Kolia and Anuta and their children would be invited each year so Kolia could conduct the service. As time went by, the Landes' son and son-in-law took over the conducting of the Passover Seder.

The Lande family eventually opened a successful dress shop. Their oldest daughter, Bella, and her husband, Harry, went into the same business. After World War II, contact with the Lande family ebbed.

Work was plentiful but, except for Misha, no one had a skill. Kolia found a job in a factory making brass beds where he was taught to be a metal worker assembling the bed frames. After a while, he smashed his thumb, leaving him with a misshapen fingernail. Anuta worked in a retail shop, Elieser got a job with an electrician who taught him the trade, and Misha worked on the Yiddish newspaper, *Forvitz* (Forward).

A short time after arrival in the United States, a decision was made to anglicize the family's names. Nikolai became Nicolas, Anuta was now Anita, Elieser became Leo and Misha was called Morris. Many years later, when the spelling of Verozub was changed to Verosub, Nicolas changed the spelling of his name to Nicholas. The patronymic names of Kolia, Anuta and Misha continued to be used by the immediate family. At about the same time, it was decided that everyone should attend night school to learn English. After they completed the short course, Kolia continued to take classes and received a Certificate of Literacy in October, 1923. He had gotten his Citizenship Certificate in June, 1923, and now, with the Literacy Certificate, he would be able to vote.

In April, 1917, America declared war on Germany. Kolia had become a metal worker and the steel mills were hiring people, so he and Anuta moved to Allentown, Pennsylvania. Kolia received a notice from the Selective Service Board on the 8th of August, 1917, to report for induction on the 15th, but he was discharged on the 24th of August because he wore glasses.

When he arrived in New York, Misha needed a place to live. How he located Mania and Israel Garskoff, originally from Kiev where Israel worked as a carpenter in Lieb Golostupitz's (Misha's father's) woodworking shop, is unknown. Although the Garskoffs had five sons and two daughters, they somehow found room for Misha to live with them. Many years later, the youngest son related the fact that he had originally thought Misha was one of his brothers. The oldest daughter, Anna, married Paul Volchok on her "Sweet Sixteen" birthday on December 25th, 1919, then was taken from the reception hall to a local hospital for an emergency appendectomy. Through the years, the Volchok family was very much involved with the Verosub and Golos families.

In the meantime, Leo met a young lady, Hattie, in New York, and they were married in the fall of 1917. Hattie had been born in America, and she was unhappy with the foreign sounding name of "Verozub." She prevailed upon Leo to anglicize the family name. Since they lived near a street called "Vernon" and the first three letters of both names were the same, Leo felt comfortable with Vernon as a family name and had the name changed legally in 1918.

In November, 1918, the armistice was signed and things slowed down economically in the United States, including in the steel mills where Kolia and Anuta worked, so they returned to

New York and took an apartment on Clinton Street on the lower East Side of Manhattan.

The year 1919 was an eventful one for the family. Hattie and Leo had a son, born on February 27th, and they named him Murray. Misha met Fannie, and they were married on November 15th. The name "Golostuptiz" was shortened to "Golos," meaning voice in Russian. On December 27th, Anuta and Kolia had a son who they named Bernard (that's me). And two other people became part of the family.

Just how the family met Jan Dudaryk-Kaminsky is not known. Since Kolia, Anuta and Misha were members of a Russian club, it is possible that they met there. Fannie was a sewing machine operator and member of the International Ladies Garment Workers Union, and she may have met Celia while working in one of the shops. There is also the possibility that Misha and Jan met while working at the Russian newspaper called *Novy Mir*[4]. Celia and Jan hold a very special place in the memories of the Verosub-Golos families. Jan was born in Bialystok, Poland, in 1895 and migrated to America in 1913 via Bremen on the SS Salamanca. Prior to meeting the family in 1919, he had worked in the Wilkes Barre, Pennsylvania coal mines; Pittsburgh, Pennsylvania steel mills; and the Baltimore, Maryland B & O Railroad yards. At the time he met the family, he was a linotype operator. Celia had been born in Yednitze, Bessarabia in 1895, and she too came to America in 1913. Jan and Celia were married on January 24, 1920, just after Jan was released from a detention camp[5] on Ellis Island on January 20th. Upon his release, he changed his family name from Dudaryk to Kaminsky.

---

[4]*Novy Mir* was a magazine published in New York City by Russian émigrés. For a short time, Leon Trotsky was a contributor.

[5]In the latter part of 1919, a US Attorney General named Mitchell Palmer believed that all people of Russian descent were Bolsheviks (Communists) planning to overthrow the US government. He had his deputies raid Russian clubs, newspapers and so on, which became known as Palmer Raids. Anyone picked up was taken to Ellis Island and deported. I, Bernie, was born on December 27th, and eight days later (on a Sunday), the family and close friends attended the traditional Bris (circumcision) ritual. That morning, the Russian club where the family were members was raided. Jan usually went

In 1921, Anuta, Kolia, Fannie and Misha relocated from the lower East Side to Harlem. My earliest recollection was a tenement building on 111th Street and Fifth Avenue. We lived very close to Central Park, which ends at 110th Street and Fifth Avenue, and Misha and Fannie had an apartment in the same building. Hattie, Leo and Murray moved to the eastern part of uptown Bronx. Kolia returned to the brass bed factory to work, Misha worked on the Yiddish newspapers (at that time, there were three) and on *Novy Mir*, and Fannie was a sewing machine operator in the dress industry and an active member of Local 22 of the International Garment Workers Union. (Years later, she became an organizer for the union. By this time, Fannie, Misha and Leo had become members of the American Communist Party.)[6] Anuta and Hattie stayed home taking care of their babies.

I have a number of memories of growing up in these neighborhoods. When I was four years old, we lived in Harlem on 111th Street and Fifth Avenue. I can't remember why, but a neighbor kid hit me with a stick with a protruding nail, and the nail went into the upper part of my lip right under my nose and made a big hole. We rushed to our friend, Dr. Sophie Lock, who

---

there on Sundays, but instead attended my Bris. Everyone at the Russian club had been arrested and deported. Shortly after the Bris, Jan was arrested at the newspaper. In the meantime, a hue and cry was made about the deportations which forced Palmer to stop the raids, and all the people in detention camps were released. All through the years, Jan would say to me, "By golly, Bernard, if it wasn't for you, I would not be in America today." Thus, Jan always claimed that I helped him remain in America. Our association with the Kaminskys became very close and an important part of our family life.

[6]The American Communist Party started in Chicago in 1919, later moving to New York. Before 1925, membership was approximately 2,400, organized into 36 neighborhood and union groups in the needle, metal, and building trades, and in the printing, railroad, and food industries. The party later fought racial discrimination in factories. In the 1930s, the Party organized the unemployed and protested evictions and cuts in relief, and Communism's popularity increased among artists, writers, and intellectuals. After the 1989 disintegration of the Soviet Union, prominent party members split off and formed the Committees of Correspondence. A small Chicago Communist Party remained at the close of the twentieth century.

took care of it immediately. I've never forgotten the incident because I have a scar which is still visible.

When we lived in the Van Corlandt Park section of the Bronx, there was a walkway about four blocks long with a slight hill that went from where we lived to the lake. In the winter months, it was the most wonderful thing in the world for Lennie, Ira, Rubia and I to sled down this hill, all the way straight to the lake. The Park Department would pile a huge amount of snow just before the lake so that if you went down the hill and couldn't stop, you went into the pile of snow rather than the lake.

With the arrival of 1923, the family again increased in size. Another Kolia (Nicholas) Verozub, this one the son of Aaron Verozub, arrived in New York City, having left Kiev in 1916 and traveled across Siberia to Vladivostak, then across the Pacific Ocean to Seattle, Washington. Leo and Hattie had a second son named Victor on February 26, 1923. In the spring, Octavius (Anuta and Misha's brother) arrived from Paris, changing his name to Octave and adopting the shortened name of Golos.

At this point, I deviate from my history to introduce a number of families that have become part of our extended family. Many are long-distance relatives and others, friends. The relationships were very close and, over the years, Mother and I would refer to some of their offspring as our nieces and nephews. I already mentioned the Kaminskys. Earlier I mentioned Anna and Paul Volchok who were married just before I was born. They had two sons, Lester and Herbert. After World War II, Lester moved to California, so we had very little contact with him. Herbert, a nuclear scientist, was involved with the government nuclear radiation monitoring program and lived in New Jersey. He married Ethel, and they had five children.

In the early part of 1923, an uncle of Anuta's, Hyman Golostupitz (Hymie), a brother to Lieb Golostupitz, arrived in America. For whatever reason, the immigration official at Ellis Island wrote Hymie's name on the entry document as Goloub, so he continued using the name. A sister of his also arrived, and she married and went to Canada. Hymie met a lady whose name was Olga Gorky. Her mother and Mania Garskoff were sisters. Olga and Hymie were married and over the years had a daughter and a son. At the same time that Hymie arrived, a nephew of his, Jack

Edison (an anglicized name, original not known) arrived in America. He was introduced to Olga's sister, Jennie (later changed to Jean). Jennie and her husband, Giesha Gittleman, had married in 1918 and had a daughter Mildred who was born in December of 1919. Like the Patlachs (this family is mentioned later in the 1926 segment), the Gittlemans had returned to the Soviet Union expecting to find that life would be much better than under the Czarist regime, but realized that America was the better place, and so they returned in 1923. Shortly after their return, they had a son, Irving. Much later, his name was changed to Gene Gitelle. In the late 1930s, Jennie divorced her husband and married Jack Edison. Jennie's daughter, Mildred, married Paul Glotzer and they had a son, David. The Glotzer family has had very close ties to Mother and me over the years.

A large segment of the family migrated to Philadelphia, Pennsylvania. Esther Golostupitz (my grandmother) had eight sisters. In 1905, two of her sisters, Ida Comerofsky and Edith Nebelitsky, left Russia with their husbands and children and went to America, through Ellis Island. They decided to settle in Philadelphia because Samuel Comerofsky (Samuel Comroe) had a brother living there. The Comroe family consisted of Ida and Samuel and their children Rose, Sara, Joseph, Jenny and Leah. Two sons, Albert and Herman (affectionately known as Shrimp), were born in the United States. More about this family later.

Edith Nebelitsky and her husband (name not recalled) had two children, Albert and Yetta. They first settled in Philadelphia and, after World War I, moved to Collingswood, New Jersey. There was very little contact with this family.

In the Fall of 1923, Kolia and Anuta decided to go into the restaurant business. They found a very large, ground floor apartment on 111th Street. The two rooms in front were converted into the dining area. The kitchen was used for the restaurant and for the family. Kolia, Anuta, Bernard, Octave and Kolia resided in the remaining rooms. Anuta cooked for the restaurant, and Kolia shopped and waited on tables. Octave had no difficulty getting a job designing fur coats with a manufacturer, continuing until the Fall of 1924. Kolia (Aaron's son) got a job driving a truck for a milk company. He would leave for work at midnight and come home eight o'clock the next morning. One day he arrived home with a puppy, just as we were having breakfast. The puppy nipped at everyone's feet. I got into bed and refused to have anything to do with the dog, establishing my feelings of not liking dogs. When Kolia left for work that night, the dog went with him.

In the Spring of 1924, Kolia and Leo received the sad news that their father, Reuben, had passed away. The restaurant venture did not prove to be a successful one, so in the Fall of 1924, Kolia and Anuta moved to Seagate, one of the first gated private communities in the United States, at the tip of Coney Island, a seashore resort area in Brooklyn, New York City. The area is now fenced off from Coney Island and has to be entered through a gate that is controlled by a security person. Their large rental apartment, with four bedrooms, was on the second floor of a two family house. Fannie, Misha, Octave, Kolia, Anuta and Bernie lived very comfortably in this apartment.

In 1925, Celia and Jan Kaminsky moved to Seagate not too far from our apartment. At that time, I only spoke Russian. In many Jewish homes, the house language was Yiddish, but in our home the language was Russian. When we were on the beach, Jan would use the wet sand as a blackboard and would teach me the Russian Cyrillic alphabet. One of Jan's and Celia's neighbors was a dentist, Celia Feinstein. Dr. Feinstein had been recently divorced from her husband and had two daughters, Elizabeth and Katherine (born in December, 1919, like me), and a son, Misha. All three of the children spoke Russian, and we became very good friends. Celia was looking for someone to rent her spare room, so the Kaminskys introduced Octave to Dr. Feinstein. He rented the room and a romance developed. Many years later, they were married and the Feinstein children became our cousins. On July 9, 1925, my sister, Rubia, was born. In the Fall, Jan and Celia moved to Bensonhurst, which wasn't too far from Seagate.

In March, 1925, the extended family was enlarged when my father met a family that was arriving from the Soviet Union. This was the Patlach family, Sonia (Sophie), Nyusa (Nathan), and their children, Leon and Jeannette, who had arrived in the United States in 1915. Their son, Leon, was born in 1916, and their daughter, Jeannette, in 1920. The revolution had taken place in 1917, and many Russian immigrants received letters from their families that life under the new government was much better, so the Patlach family went back in 1923. They didn't find things to be very good, and so they returned to the United States in 1925, living with our family until the fall of that year.

In September, Jeannette, Katherine and I started attending school. Our parents were not aware that children at the age of five began school by attending kindergarten, so we started in the first grade when all three of us would turn six before the end of the year. The three of us had a very difficult time because none of us spoke English. We all went home and told our parents that from now on we would only speak English.

1926 was a very sad year for Hattie and Leo Vernon. Their son, Victor, who was a little more than three years old, died on June 3, 1926. Leo felt Hattie had neglected the baby, causing his death.

At the end of the summer in 1927, the family made some drastic changes. Kolia and Anuta moved to the Mosholu Parkway area of the Bronx and rented a four-room apartment at 3475 Knox Place, on the corner of Gun Hill Road and Knox Place. The following year, Celia, Jan and their son, Lucian, moved into the same building. Fannie and Misha moved to Shakespeare Avenue in the Bronx, which was located around 167th Street. In November, Leo and Hattie separated and, for a short time, Leo and Murray lived with Anuta and Kolia. After Leo's and Hattie's divorce was final, Hattie got custody of Murray and Leo moved in with Fannie and Misha. The Patlach family were also living in the same Mosholu Parkway area, as were the Volchoks.

Fannie had become an important person in the Communist Party of America. In November of 1927, the Soviet Union was celebrating the Tenth Anniversary of the Russian Revolution. Fannie was invited as one of the honored guests from America. She had never met the family in Kiev, so she planned to go to Kiev after the festivities in Moscow. Before she left America, it was decided that the entire family would get together and have a picture taken so she could bring it with her. Kolia, Anuta, Rubia, Bernie, Octave, Leo, Misha and Fannie went to the photography studio, and it was a very happy occasion. During Aunt Fannie's visit to the Soviet Union, the big joke in the family was that

Uncle Misha and Uncle Leo had only bought soap and oranges while she was gone.

Upon returning from the Soviet Union, Aunt Fannie gave me a yarmulka that had been made by my Aunt Dvera, Kolia's sister. At the time I'm writing this story (eighty-three years later), I still have the yarmulka in my possession. Although it is customary for Jewish sons to begin Cheder (Hebrew School) to prepare for the Bar Mitzvah, Kolia was determined that the family become Americanized so they would never be persecuted as they had been in Russia. Therefore, he refused to become a member of any Temple or Shul or attend religious services. However, after Rubia turned five and I was ten, we would sit down with Kolia each month to learn about the customs, holidays, and history of the Jewish people.

Kolia (Aaron Verozub's son) met Sarah Zalkin, and they were married in March, 1927. Wearing a top hat and tails, I was the ring bearer at their wedding. Shortly after the wedding, Kolia was offered a supervisory job by a milk distributing company and the family relocated to Wilkes Barre, Pennsylvania where they resided for the rest of their years, never having children. From time to time, the families would get together.

In Philadelphia, the Comroe family was also expanding. Aunt Ida (Meema) and Uncle Sam's children married. Rose married Ralph Rosenthal[7] who was a plumbing contractor. Ida and Sam's son, Joe, married Mary and had two daughters, Marion and Ruth. Shrimp married Lillian and had a son, Steven. Al was married to Marge. Shrimp and Al became electrical contractors. Leah married Louis Levine[8], and they had an appliance store. Much later, Jennie married a man named Sam. Sara married Herman Schwartz in March, 1927. Herman was a pharmacist, opening a drug store in north Philadelphia. The early years were difficult, and Herm worked as a cab driver after he closed the store at 9:00 in the evening. Sara and Herm had two children, Joan and Phillip.

---

[7] They had two daughters, Sylvia and Ada. Years later, in 1942, I lived with Sylvia and her husband, Dave, while attending a Signal Corps School, and after Mother and I married, we lived with them for a short time.

[8] They had a daughter, Ann, who married Lenny Brown. They reside in the Atlanta, Georgia, area.

Joan was born in December, 1929, and Phil was born in July, 1933. The Verosub and Golos families were close to Sara and Herm. For many years, we would visit them either at Christmas or Passover. Unfortunately, a short time after Joan's birth, Sara and Herm were told by the doctor (Herm's brother) that Joan was retarded. In later years, this caused some serious situations for Sara and Herm. During the period of time that Mother and I resided in Philadelphia (1942-1944), we would visit the Schwartzes at least three or four times a week. Actually, it was Herm who taught me how to operate a business, and I used many of his suggestions in later years. On one of our visits around 1950, Sara and Herm discussed Joan's care with us, should something happen to Sara and Herm. We agreed to become Joan's guardian if this situation developed, but the issue never arose even after Herm died in the late 1950s. Their son, Phil, married Elaine, and they had three sons, one son passing away at a young age. The Comroe family had wonderful genes. Meema died at the age of 105. Although Albert died at a young age, all of his sisters and brothers were 95 or older when they passed away. Sara died at the age of 105 in 2003, and Joan died two months later at the age of 74. As of now, Leah is still alive and is about 105 years old.

1927 was an important year for Uncle Misha. The Communist Party had published a number of newspapers in different languages, and a decision was made to concentrate the efforts on the English and Yiddish papers. At the same time, the Party purchased a building with an entrance on Twelfth and Thirteenth streets between Broadway and University Place that was one block long. The printing plant was to be located on the seventh floor, with the editorial offices for the *Daily Worker* on the eighth floor. *The Morning Freiheit* (Freedom), the Yiddish paper, would have editorial offices on the sixth floor, and the printing presses were located in the basement. The National offices were on the ninth floor, and the New York offices were on the fifth floor. On the 13th Street side, there was a bookstore. Uncle Misha was President of a printing company called F & D Printing Co., holding the position until his retirement in 1958. The Vice-President was Arthur Stein. Many years later, after Fannie and Misha's daughter, Ditta, was born, people thought the F & D stood for Fannie and Ditta. It actually stood for Freiheit and Daily.

My first job at the paper was as a floor boy. The linotype machines were used to set up the type for the newspaper, creating the major body of the text. Other hands set the headlines and put together the advertisements. This was all set into a steel frame that was the exact size of a newspaper page. When the pages were completed, they were taken to a special press where a treated cardboard mat was placed on the form. The form was rolled through the press, and the entire page was impressed with the mat, which was then sent to the press room. Half round metal plates were made and placed on the drums of the presses. As a floor boy, there were many jobs to be done, such as sweeping the floor, moving the galleys of type around, making proofs of the type for the proofreaders, moving the page forms from the handset area to the mat press, etc. The final step came after the paper had been completely run off the presses --the type would be thrown into small hand trucks and taken to the smelting room where the lead slugs were shoveled into a huge pot and melted into a liquid. The liquid was run into forms that were half round and about one-and-a-half inches wide by twenty-four inches long with an eyelet at the top. These pigs, as they were called, were hung into the linotype machine and supplied the lead for the type.

There were about eight boys, most over eighteen, working in the shop at that time. The printers were all members of the Typographical Union (Big 6), and they had strict rules as to who could handle the type. The older fellows were militant members of the Young Communist League (YCL) who thought that a floor boys union would get us more recognition. Groups of us would visit the other newspapers and printing shops and, in a very short time, we were able to form the floor boys union. Our success had two effects. First, we were able to negotiate a contract and received a pay raise from forty-cents an hour to seventy-five cents an hour. Then, in 1940, the typographical union thought two unions in one area of a printing company might be detrimental to the industry, so they suggested making our union a junior part of theirs. This was acceptable to us, and the merger was made, which proved to be a wise decision. (When I visited the print shop in 1952, I was surprised to learn that the worker doing my job was getting nine dollars an hour and had a month's vacation time each year.) Arthur Stein, the co-owner of the F & D Printing Co., suggested that I also work in the office. He taught me how to do bookkeeping and make up payrolls and, eventually, how to prepare income tax returns. I was able to supplement my income by preparing the income tax returns for the people who worked for the printing company and, many years later, this proved to be a great help in preparing the various tax returns for Mother's and my business.

Through the years, those of us in the second generation were never aware of the high positions that Uncle Misha and Aunt Fannie held in the American Communist Party. It wasn't until 1935 when I went to work at their printing shop that I found out about their status. In the early years, Uncle Leo was a minor member of the Party, however in 1939 when he and Aunt Bella went to New Jersey to live on a chicken farm, his work became very important. The cell to which he belonged worked to organize chicken farmers into two cooperatives. One was called FEPCO, Farm Egg Producers Co-Op. The co-op trucks would pick up the boxes of eggs from the farmers and sell them to the large supermarket chains. The second co-op was FLF: Freehold, Lakewood, Farmingdale Co-Op. There was a union called District 65 in New York City which represented the retail salespeople throughout the city and was Communist-dominated. Uncle Leo and the members of his cell were instrumental in arranging the financing of the FLF through District 65, which provided all the funds for the purchase of land with a railroad siding, the construction of four huge silos and many other buildings. The FLF became the major feed company in the Farmingdale-Lakewood-Freehold area. All during this time, there wasn't any stigma attached to being a Communist. Although the Soviet Union was not recognized until 1933 and ambassadors exchanged, people could openly talk about their membership. After the Stalin-Hitler pact in 1939, the Communists fell into disfavor with the American people; however, when the Soviet Union entered World War II on the side of the Allies, things eased up a great deal. In 1954, America outlawed the Communist Party on the basis that it was planning to overthrow the United

States government. The Senator McCarthy[9] hearings also caused the Communist Party to be looked upon with great disfavor.

In the late 1920s and into the 1930s, the economic status of the family had its ups and downs. When the family moved to the Bronx in 1927, Kolia left his job in the brass bed factory to work in the fur industry. His first job was working for a company that made fur collars and cuffs for women's cloth coats. At first he did odd jobs in the shop, but after a while he became a salesman. He would visit the coat manufacturers to get them to order their collars and cuff sets from his company. Misha worked in the printing industry on the Russian and Yiddish newspapers. Their friend from Paris, Abraham Lomaskin, had formed a printing company in 1923 with four other men, and he invited Misha to join the group. Since all the partners could do different jobs, there weren't any employees. This was beneficial when there was a general strike in the printing industry a few years later, and their shop was able to operate because there were no employees. The company, Georgian Press, eventually became a major company in the New York printing industry.

Leo had left his electrician's job and gone to work in the men's clothing industry. For a short time, he became a cutter of men's suits. In 1928, he met a young lady, Bella Likorenko, from Novgorod, Russia, at one of the Russian clubs where the family were members. They married in March, 1929. At this time, Bella worked as a seamstress in a well-known fashionable ladies shop called Hattie Carnegie. The months of March to July were very busy in this industry, so they postponed their honeymoon until August when they planned to go to Europe and the Soviet Union to see both families. In 1928, Leo had become

---

[9]Joseph Raymond "Joe" McCarthy (1908 – 1957) was a Republican Senator from the state of Wisconsin from 1947 until his death in 1957. Beginning in 1950, McCarthy became the public face when Cold War tensions fueled fears of widespread Communist subversion. He was noted for making claims that there were large numbers of Communists and Soviet spies and sympathizers inside the federal government and elsewhere. Ultimately, his tactics and his inability to substantiate his claims led him to be censured by the United States Senate.

involved with the stock market. He would sit at the Stock Exchange on Wall Street and buy and sell stocks daily. At that time, one could buy stocks on margin and needed very little money as collateral. In October, 1929, the stock market crashed while he and Bella were in the Soviet Union, and he was completely wiped out. For some unknown reason, they had only purchased one-way tickets. In order for Bella and Leo to return to America, Kolia and Misha had to send them money to purchase return trip tickets since, in 1929, credit cards and traveler checks were unknown. Having lost all their money in the stock market crash, they were invited to become part of the Verosub-Golos household.

After the crash, Leo bought a panel body truck and would buy an assortment of cookies from the baking companies, reselling them to small grocery and dairy stores. This lasted for just a short while, and until Leo joined Kolia and another man in their fur manufacturing company, named Vero Bros. and Rynd. About 1934, Leo went back to the men's clothing industry as a cutter of men's suits.

Octave worked as a fitter and later as a designer in many different shops that manufactured fur coats until around 1930 when he opened his own business as a fur coat designer. Since there were many fur coat manufacturers that could not afford to have a designer on staff, a customer would go to Octave's shop where he would prepare a fabric copy of the coat design and make the pattern. He also would work up designs and make patterns in different sizes that were sold to manufacturers for mass production of fur coats. In 1940, Anuta went to work in Octave's office as a receptionist.

Jan continued to work in the printing industry, first on various Russian language papers. In the 1930s, he went to work for the Prompt Press Company which was a job printing shop owned by the Communist Party. This company printed all sorts of magazines, pamphlets, etc. in various languages, including English. As a linotype operator, Jan could set type in all the Slavic languages as well as in English. Paul Volchok worked as the manager of a ladies lingerie shop for a chain of stores called the Lerner Shops. In the mid 1930s, he opened his own store on Broadway and 104th Street.

Now to return to the chronological story. It was Spring of 1929 when Fannie and Misha informed the family that Fannie was expecting a baby in August. A decision was made for Anuta, Kolia and the children to move into a large apartment with Fannie and Misha. Down the street at 3425 Knox Place, they found an apartment with three bedrooms and two bathrooms, plus a living room, dining room and kitchen. The foyer or hall was large enough to be made into a dining room, allowing the dining room to be used as a bedroom. Each couple had a bedroom, I had a room for myself, and Rubia and the baby shared a room. Fannie had read a trilogy of books by a Danish author, Martin Andersen Nexo (*Ditte Girl Alive, Ditte Toward the Stars*, and *Ditte Daughter of Man*), and was fascinated by the heroine in the three stores. She decided that, boy or girl, the baby's name would be Ditte.

On August 14, 1929, a baby girl arrived, and Fannie changed the spelling to "Ditta." The families are to be congratulated for choosing the names "Rubia" and "Ditta," as they are unique. I have never met anyone with either name, although in our tour group in Asia, an Austrian woman from Vienna was named "Dita." At one time, I read about a woman from the Colorado area whose first name was Ditta. In Italian, the word "dita" means sons. In our Philadelphia branch of the family, one of the great granddaughters of my Great-Aunt Ida Comroe was named Ditta.

These were happy times for Rubia and me. Fannie returned to work and her activities about a week after Ditta was born, and Anuta took care of Rubia, Ditta and me. It was like having a baby sister in the house. All through the years, the relationship between Ditta, Rubia and me was mixed-up. Like any siblings, we teased and made fun of one another and did things to get one angry at the other.[10]

---

[10] In 1947, Ditta married a young man named Phillip Oliker, and they had 3 sons, Steven, David and Robert. When the third son was about 6 years old, Phillip decided he wanted a divorce. Ditta was forced to make a decision: go to work or go to school. She decided work was essential because Phil did not provide sufficient or timely funds for the family. After a while, Aunt Fannie and Uncle Misha encouraged Ditta to go to college, which she did. She received a doctorate in clinical psychology when she was 50 years old. Today,

In 1929, the stock market crash caused a monumental depression all through the world. Overall, the family was fortunate. Misha, as head of a printing company, was secure in his job. Jan managed continuous employment in the printing industry. Bella always seemed to have work in the Hattie Carnegie shop. Fannie was working in many shops in order to get a full week's work. Kolia worked in a shop that manufactured fur trimmings for cloth coats. Besides being a salesperson, he learned how to work with fur. This enabled him to have full weeks of work. Leo had bought a panel body truck and was involved in the cookie business.

Evidently, the family did not experience a financial crunch since we went to a summer resort every summer, the earliest that I can remember being 1927. We stayed on 95th Street in Rockaway Beach, New York. The place was called the Lester House and was owned by Mania and Izzy Garskoff, the people with whom Misha lived upon his arrival in America. The hotel was named after their grandson, Lester, the son of Anna and Paul Volchok. Here I had my first job, at the age of seven-and-a-half, with Lenny Kaplan[11]. We set the tables for three meals a day, every day, all through the summer. On Labor Day weekend, one of Mania's sons took Lenny and me to the Rockaway Playland Amusement Park. We each got five rides and were given twenty-five cents in cash. In 1927, a ride at the amusement park cost one

---

she is doing well with a successful practice, and she has written a book on psychology, <u>Hide & Seek: Reclaiming Childhood's Lost Potential.</u> She never remarried and takes advantage of her free time by traveling with friends. In 1973, David was on a camping trip with three of his friends in Henry Cowell Redwoods State Park in California when they were shot to death by serial killer Herbert Williams Mullin. Mullin was eventually sentenced to life imprisonment and is still behind bars at Mule Creek State Prison, in Ione, California. Mullin was turned down for parole (for the tenth time) in March, 2006, and is eligible to ask for a parole hearing again in 2011. Each time Mullin's parole comes up, Robert and Steven attend the parole hearing and protest the release. Steven now produces shows for corporate annual report meetings, and Robert is an attorney, both in California.

[11] Lenny's parents were Anna and Aaron Kaplan, and Uncle Aaron was a brother to Mania Garskoff and Mrs. Gorky. Lenny had two brothers, Milton and Ira.

nickel. I immediately put the quarter into my mouth for safekeeping and swallowed it. Upon my return to the hotel, I was given a good dose of a laxative.

In 1928, Anuta, Celia and the children spent the summer on a farm owned by the Geiselhart family in Napanoch, New York, in the Catskill Mountains. The working members of the family came up Wednesday evening and for the weekend. In the early 1930s, the family returned to Rockaway Beach. One summer, Kolia Verosub (son of Aaron Verosub) and his wife, Sara, shared a bungalow with Anuta, Kolia and the children. Another eventful summer, Fannie, Misha, Anuta, Kolia, Anna and Paul Volchok and five children shared a huge apartment on the second floor of a large two-family house.

For a number of years, the family spent the summer in Rockaway Beach at a hotel called "Resnikoff's," adjacent to the beach. The front porch had originally been part of the boardwalk, but when a large segment of the boardwalk burned down, it was necessary to construct a new one. The area of the boardwalk in front of the hotel was in good condition, so the ends were closed and it became the hotel porch where we could walk down the steps and stroll into the ocean. With all our friends and relatives around, it was a great place to spend the summer.

The hotel had about twenty-five rooms, and each couple had a room. Two additional rooms were rented, one for the boys and one for the girls. The hotel had been converted into a "Koch Alayn" (Yiddish for cook alone). Each family had a table and chairs, plus a server, which contained dishes and utensils. The community kitchen had about fifteen stoves and twenty cupboards where groceries were kept under lock and key. On the back porch, there were a like number of ice boxes which were also locked. At dinner time, the children would march around the dining room and survey what was being served. If one of the other families had a meal more to their liking, it wasn't much of a problem to get invited for dinner. Across from the hotel there was a refreshment stand. The big treat would be a large pitcher of cherry-coke soda that cost ten cents.

In the 1930s, the families decided to make some changes. During the depression years (1929-1939), apartments were plentiful and readily available. When a lease ended, people would look for a new apartment because it would eliminate the need to have your apartment painted and, since there were an abundance of apartments, the landlords would allow one or two months concession on the rent. In 1930, the Verosub family moved to 3467 DeKalb Avenue[12], and Bella and Leo moved to 3457 DeKalb Avenue. The Golos and Kaminsky families moved to Brooklyn. They settled in Brighton Beach, the Goloses on Humboldt Street and the Kaminskys on Humbert Street and then Ripple Street.

In 1932, the families joined forces and moved to Manhattan where they lived at 561 West 141st Street. While the Goloses and the Kaminskys lived in Brighton Beach (1931-33), the Verosub family spent the summer in Manhattan Beach, adjacent to Brighton Beach. In 1934-35, the summers were again spent in Rockaway at the Resnikoff Hotel.

The Verosubs kept moving in the Mosholu Parkway area and, in 1931, moved to 3569 DeKalb Avenue where we were joined in the building by the Patlach family and Bella and Leo. The Patlach family opened a small dairy store on Gun Hill Road, located across the way from my school, Public School 94. Each morning when Rubia and I went to school, I would go around the corner to a bakery on Jerome Avenue, the main business street, and buy two-dozen rolls for twenty-four cents (actually, twenty-six rolls since a baker's dozen is thirteen rolls). On my way to school, I would bring the rolls to the Patlaches' store. Every day at lunchtime, I would go to the store with Rubia and Jeannette. Since our house was about eight blocks from the school, this was a very convenient arrangement.

---

[12]The Kaplan family moved to 3457 DeKalb Avenue. Since the summer of 1927 when Lenny and I worked for Mania Garskoff, Lenny and I would see each other from time to time. Shortly after school began in 1930, we both resumed our friendship on a full-time basis and met Stanley Rapport. The three of us became inseparable until World War II, and whenever you saw two of us, the third was not far away. After the war, Stan's family moved to California, and we lost track of him. My association with Lenny continued until he passed away. Sometime in the 1970s, Stan and his wife May came east for an event, and we re-established our friendship. Stan has since passed away, and May is living with her daughter.

In 1933, we moved to 3525 Rochambeau Avenue. As far as Rubia and I were concerned, all this moving around did not affect our schooling. All these addresses were in the same school district. In 1932, when I was in the sixth grade, I graduated from Public School 94 and was sent to Creston Junior High School, which was on 181st Street and Creston Avenue. At that time, the year was split into two terms, A and B, however, in the junior high schools, grades 7A and 7B were in the fall term and grades 8A and 8B were in the spring term. The ninth year was also spent in junior high school. In 1934, I graduated from Creston and went into DeWitt Clinton High School which was in a park in the Mosholu-Woodlawn area. Rubia went to P.S. 94 and continued on at P.S. 80, then went to Hunter High School in midtown Manhattan. During this period of time, Ditta and Lucian went to schools in the area of Manhattan where they lived. Later on, when the families moved back to the Bronx, they went to the same schools as Rubia and I did.

Around 1933 or 1934, the family became involved with an organization called the International Workers Order (IWO), an ethnic fraternal organization. The individual lodges were made up of various nationalities such as Slovak, Russian, French, Jewish, Italian, Polish and American. One of the reasons for joining was the benefits that members received, like low-cost term life insurance policies and burial grounds. The IWO had a medical program that was the forerunner of two medical plans, HIP in New York and the Kaiser Plan in California. They also had a medical plan called "The Plan for Plenty." It was introduced in Congress by New York Congressman Vito Marcantonio, and Medicare is based on this plan.

The IWO also sponsored social activities and programs for the children. The lodge to which the family belonged had a Drum and Bugle Corps that Leo supervised. As members, Lucian, Ditta and Rubia participated in a competition at the 1939 New York World's Fair, and I worked as a volunteer organizer of youth clubs in Harlem in New York City. Later, during the 1950s McCarthy era, the IWO was declared to be a Communist organization and was forced to disband, and various state insurance boards took over the administration of the insurance and burial policies.

1933 was the beginning of a new era for the families' second generation. I was the eldest, so at 13-1/2 years of age, I went to work during the summers of 1933 and 1934 for Uncle Octave at his fur business on Seventh Avenue between 30th and 31st Streets in Manhattan. After Octave made the muslin fabric copy of a fur coat that he had designed for a customer, he would take it apart. My job was to place all the units on large sheets of heavy brown paper, trace the units onto the paper, and cut them out. These patterns would then be sent to a coat manufacturer to use in making the coat. Stock patterns were also made, and the median size was 12. By the end of the summer, I was able to grade patterns up or down without any problem. My pay was forty cents an hour.

In 1935, the families were on the move again. The Golos family moved back to the Bronx at the beginning of the summer, joining the Verosub family in a very large two-bedroom apartment at 3424 DeKalb Avenue, so that Ditta would begin first grade in the new school in the fall. The foyer was made into a dining room, and the dining room became a bedroom. There were sleeper couches in one bedroom and the living room. The move was convenient for both families since Fannie and Misha saved on the cost of having a housekeeper, and Anuta and Kolia reduced the cost of their rent. Celia, Jan and Lucian remained in Manhattan. They moved to an apartment near Broadway and 169th Street. Bella and Leo moved into the same area.

In 1936, the Verosub and Golos families moved again, and the summer was spent in Seagate, in the same apartment that we had rented in 1925. That summer, the first floor apartment was occupied by the Lomaskin Family. Over the years, the families would get together from time to time, speaking Russian and a small amount of Yiddish.

The Seagate summer of 1936 was the beginning of a new phase in my life. One of the neighbors had a visiting niece, Ruth Gelb from East Orange, for the summer. A friendship developed and, at the end of the summer, we exchanged addresses. During the course of the winter, I would go to New Jersey to date Ruth where I met a large group of fellows who were dating Ruth's girlfriends. Ruth and I decided to part company in 1940 following a New Year's Eve party where words were exchanged, but three guys from this group became good friends -- Dave Levee, his nephew, Henny Levee, and Saul Lipman. While not as close as the relationship I had with Lenny Kaplan and Stan Rapport, the friendship has lasted through the years. When Vera and I went into business in 1947, Dave was a salesman for a large hardware supplier and helped set up the stock for the store. Henny and I were involved in the manufacture of drop leaf tables for small kitchens, I producing and Henny selling them. In years to come, Saul would become my brother-in-law.

The Golos family spent the summer of 1937 at Golden's Bridge in New York State, and the Verosub family visited a few weekends. In September of that year, I graduated from DeWitt Clinton High School and was enrolled in New York University College of Engineering, tuition being $175 a semester. Anyone who excelled in a particular subject and took it for four years with a grade of 95 or better in each of the Regent's exams would be granted a $100/year scholarship, which meant that tuition would be only $250 for the year. I won one of these scholarships.

Isaac Werosub received his visa in 1937 and came to America to live with the Verosub and Golos families. Finally, on February 22, 1938, his wife Zinaida and daughter Victoria, born in June, 1923, in Danzig arrived in New York, but not without some drama.

Isaac Verosub had left Russia in 1918 and gone to Poland, becoming the director of the local HIAS office in Danzig. The city of Danzig, at the end of World War I, was created as a free city to give Poland access to the Baltic Sea. Isaac quickly found out that the city was predominantly German; prior to World War I, it had been part of Prussia. Since the Germans didn't pronounce Vs clearly and pronounced Ws like Vs, he changed the spelling of his last name to Werosub. He supervised the HIAS staff until the 1930s when the plague of Hitlerism crept into Danzig, just like it did in other parts of Europe, and it became difficult for a Jewish person to exist there. He returned to Poland, but saw that things were getting worse there too and decided it was time to make a change. The HIAS was helpful in eventually getting him to America, but first the American government required immigrants to have an affidavit from a family member already in America vowing that they would support the new family. The only person in America who was Isaac's direct relative was his brother, Nicolas (Kolia) Verosub, who had the same name as my father. Nicolas had a job with a milk company in Wilkes Barre, Pennsylvania, but he refused to provide an affidavit. My father, only a cousin of Isaac's, and Uncle Misha, not being related at all, couldn't supply the government with the required affidavit. It was a turbulent time, with lots of phone calls back and forth to try to convince Nicolas to sign. This upset my father and Uncle Misha very much. They traveled to Pennsylvania to convince Nicolas to sign the affidavit. To help matters, my father and Misha gave Nicolas an affidavit guaranteeing that they would take care of the family.

When Zinaida and Vicki finally arrived in America, we met them at the boat. My welcome gesture to Vicki was a Hershey bar which is what the GIs later handed out in Europe at the end of World War II. We brought the family to our Bronx apartment to move in with my mother, father, sister, and I, and Aunt Fannie, Uncle Misha, and Ditta. For her first meal in America, we took Vicki to the local candy store and bought her her first ice cream soda. Shortly after, Vicki's family went to Wilkes Barre, but they soon returned to an apartment in our area on Kingsbridge Road, where Vicki attended Walton High School. When she arrived in America, Vicki had spoken German, Russian, Polish, French and a little Italian, but no English. That June, just months after arriving in America, she had the highest grade in her English class.[13] Isaac continued to work in New York City for the Hebrew Immigration Aid Society (HIAS), a very busy organization because of the thousands of Jews trying to flee from Germany.

The year 1938 was very much like the previous one, with Ditta and Lucian going to a children's camp called Camp Irendale and the rest of the family remaining in the city. The depression was still in full force, and the situation in Europe was

---

[13] The years went by, Vicki's father passed away around 1942, and she married Victor after the war, having met him while attending Brooklyn College. They had five daughters; Victor and one daughter have since passed away. Vicki is now remarried and lives in Florida in the winter and in Illinois the rest of the year.

getting worse, with Hitler and the German armies seizing Austria and Czechoslovakia. 1939 was a continuation of the year before except, in August of 1939, the Soviet Union and Germany signed a Non-Aggression Pact[14]. This created tremendous problems for family members. Those who were members of the Communist Party strictly adhered to the party policy and defended the pact. On the other hand, many of the sympathizers and party "pinks" were disillusioned. In the Verosub-Golos household, the debates were long and bitter, especially between Kolia and Fannie. On September 1, 1939, Germany, without a declaration of war, invaded Poland. Within three days, England and France joined the conflict and World War II began.

In August of 1939, Bella and Leo decided to become chicken farmers, and they bought forty acres of land in Jerseyville, New Jersey, near Freehold, New Jersey, for $3,000. The farm consisted of a house with electricity and heat, but no bathroom. The kitchen's sink had a hand pump that was connected to a well in the basement, and the waste water ran out onto the ground. The second floor had five small rooms. Two were made into a large bedroom, one was converted into a bathroom and two became small guest rooms. There was a very large decrepit barn on the farm. Sears-Roebuck was engaged to fix up the house and put in a Youngstown metal kitchen and bathroom and upgrade the heating system, at a cost of $2,000. The most important project, at a cost of $4,000, was the construction of two chicken coops, each with eleven twelve-foot by twelve-foot rooms and a

---

[14]On August 23, 1939, a little over a week before the beginning of World War II, the Nazi-Soviet Non-Aggression Pact was signed. Publicly, this agreement stated that Germany and the Soviet Union would not attack each other. The pact was supposed to last for ten years, but it lasted for less than two. If Germany attacked Poland, then the Soviet Union would not come to Poland's aid. Thus, if Germany went to war against France and Great Britain over Poland, the Soviets were guaranteeing that they would not enter the war, thus not opening a second front for Germany. There was also a secret addendum to the pact, denied by the Soviets until 1989, that they would receive the Baltic States of Estonia, Latvia, Lithuania and part of Poland as spoils of war.

basement under the first room. There were ten rooms all in a row for the chickens, with the first room being the storeroom with an egg room underneath. Each building had a capacity of 5,000 chickens, with a trolley that ran the length of the building. Leo continued to work in New York cutting men's suits, commuting to the city each day. Bella worked on the farm with a farmhand to help her.

During the summer of 1940, I often had the opportunity to go to Uncle Leo's farm. Henny was working for a venetian blind company, and he would go to the shore on Sundays to do installations. After our Saturday night dates, we would get up early on Sunday to do the installation. Then we would go back to the farm and do all sorts of jobs for Bella and Leo. I became enchanted with farm life and entertained the idea of settling on a farm. After I met Vera in 1941, she would go with me to the farm and gradually started to like the lifestyle.

Working on a chicken farm was a new experience for us, especially when we learned that chickens were vaccinated. The College of Agriculture Department at Rutgers University suggested vaccinating the chickens in order to prevent diseases from affecting fowl life, and they used my uncle's farm as an experimental station. Neighboring farmers would help one another with the vaccinations. The night before the event, the chickens were chased into the range shelters so they were ready for the early morning procedure. At 5 AM, everyone gathered at two of the range shelters. A cage would be attached to the door as it was opened, then the chickens were awakened and herded to the front of the shelter and into the cage. The top of the cage had a trap door so that the chickens could be removed one at a time. Its wing was spread out, and the serum was injected using a syringe. The fowl was then passed to another team that painted the rectum with a different serum to prevent chicken pox. The final step was to attach a solid pair of spectacles to the beak with a cotter pin. When a chicken lays an egg, there are drops of blood. If another chicken sees the red, it will peck at it. The purpose of the spectacles was to prevent the chickens from pecking one another. Usually the work was done in teams of six, two teams to a cage. When the operation was completed for the entire flock of five thousand chickens, everyone congregated at the farmhouse for a sumptuous meal.

1940 began with a tragic and traumatic event. On Friday evening, the 2nd of February, I went out for the evening with Lenny Kaplan and Stan Rapport. Fannie, Anuta, Rubia and Ditta went to see a performance of "The Blue Bird of Happiness." Misha was working his four to twelve o'clock night shift. Kolia had not yet come home from work. Returning after eleven o'clock, the ladies found the apartment door closed but unlocked. Kolia was on the bathroom floor, having committed suicide by attaching a leather belt to the shower curtain bar. His weight had pulled the bar from the wall. The police were called and, shortly afterward, Misha came home, as did I. No notes or messages with any sort of explanation were found. Paul Volchok and I did a thorough investigation into the financial records of the Vero Bros. and Rynd Co. which Kolia partly owned. No one was ever able to find anything that would explain this act of self-destruction. The funeral took place the following Sunday. Within a short time, the Verosub-Golos family moved to 3418 Gates Place.

Ditta, Rubia and Lucian were sent to Camp WoChiCa in Califon, New Jersey for the summer of 1940. While it sounds like an Indian name, the camp name was derived from the Workers Children Camp, owned and operated by the Communist Party. While at camp, Lucian[15] met Geraldine Gottlieb from Kearny, New Jersey. You might say they became an item. The Kaminskys moved back to the Bronx this year, to 3500 DeKalb Avenue. At this point, the entire family and extended members of the family lived in what was known as the Mosholu Parkway-Woodlawn Section of the Bronx.

---

[15]Lucian and I have been friends for 86 years, ever since he was born on January 30, 1926. His family lived in Bensonhurst, Brooklyn, at the time, not too far from Seagate where my family lived. Once a week, my mother would bundle up my 6-month old sister and me, and we would go to Celia's apartment because she didn't know how to take care of a child. My mother would show her how to dress and feed the baby. Lucian eventually married Geraldine and they had three sons – Peter, Robert and Donald, all married with successful careers.

The war in Europe was not going too well for the Allies. Although the United States was not directly involved in the conflict, the government decided to create a Selective Service Law[16] in September of 1940. All males 21 or older had to register. Since I was only 20 and 9 months at the registration date, I didn't have to register and my Bronx friends were younger than I, so none of them had to register. However, in New Jersey, I was the youngest by a number of years and was embarrassed to admit that I didn't have to register. I told everyone in New Jersey that I was a conscientious objector and wasn't going to register. The ruse worked and many congratulated me for having the courage of my convictions. In December, when I became 21, I registered as required. When the first draft lottery was held in the spring of 1941, only the numbers of those who registered on the original date were called to active duty.

The first of the fellows that I knew in New Jersey was drafted at the end of April, 1941. We decided to visit him on Sunday, May 4th, in Fort Dix, New Jersey. Since I didn't have a date, Henny Levee suggested that I ask Saul's sister, Vera, to be my date. It was actually a blind date, and it was the best thing that could have happened to me. Vera told me she had seen me on New Year's Eve, 1940, at Goldman's Hotel in West Orange where I had gotten a little tipsy. We hit it off well enough for me to ask for a second date, and from then on we started going more or less steady with no definite intentions. At that time, I would finish work in downtown New York, then immediately take a train to New Jersey to see Vera. She was very nice and always accepted my suggestions which not a lot of people will do with another person, which is one reason I liked her. She was good-

---

[16]The Selective Training and Service Act of 1940 was passed on September 16, 1940, establishing the first peacetime conscription in United States history. It required all males between the ages of 18 to 65 to register for Selective Service. Originally, all males aged 21 to 36 were conscripted for a service period of 12 months, but this was later increased to males aged 18 to 45 for a service period of 18 months. Upon declaration of war, the service period was extended to last the duration of the war plus a six-month service in the Organized Reserves.

looking and dressed well. Her long, dark, wavy hair was always done well, and she did it herself. She rarely went to a beauty parlor, even in later years, although in the very later years, she went every Friday. But up until maybe her 70s, she hardly ever went to a beauty parlor.

Years later, Vera told me that one of the things she liked about me was my family and family life. Our family was very close and at various times different family members lived together. At the time she met me, my father was no longer living, and we were sharing a big apartment with my Aunt Fanny and Uncle Misha and my cousin Ditta. She couldn't get over how congenial the family was, which wasn't so in her home. Her mother and father were always battling, and her father had at times hit her mother. Her parents were always having arguments with her brother because they wanted him to go to school, and he didn't want to. When he graduated from pharmacy school, he came home with his diploma and said to his mother, "Here, it's yours because you wanted me to get it. Now go hang it in the bathroom." Later on, when they bought him a liquor and drug store and he did very well, he didn't have trouble taking the money. So Vera saw this kind of life and felt that life with me would be akin to what my family life was.

Vera's mother and father had a candy store, but her father was more interested in going to boxing or wrestling matches than he was in operating the store. There was a school stadium nearby. Many times when I came out for a date, Vera's mother would find that there was an event at the stadium, and she would ask Vera and me and Vera's sister, Esther, to help in the store. The "date" ended with our making ice cream sodas or sundaes and sitting down to enjoy them together. That was the way things began.

As the summer passed, we would often go away on a weekend. Usually there was a car load of friends, and many times we went in two car loads. We would go to the Concord Hotel[17] in

---

[17]The Concord Resort Hotel was a world-famous destination in the 1950s, '60s, and '70s in the so-called Borscht Belt part of the Catskills. Located in Kiamesha Lake, New York, the Concord was the largest resort in the region, with over 1,500 guest rooms and a dining room that sat 3,000, until its closing

the Catskills on a Saturday morning and take two rooms, usually three girls in one room and the three fellows in another room. We would always have a great time at the hotel. Saturday night, there was terrific entertainment, and Sunday we spent the day swimming and having a good time, leaving in the evening.

We also did simple things at Goldman's Hotel in West Orange. This was close to home, so we didn't have to stay overnight, and it was inexpensive. We could go there on a Sunday, spend the entire day swimming, playing ball or whatever, and then have a dairy meal for Sunday night dinner. All of this cost us $5 a person. At that time, $5 was a lot, but it was still inexpensive for what we got.

Vera had never really been to New York, and so we would go on a Saturday or Sunday to various museums or sightseeing, just walking along Fifth Avenue. We sometimes went to a theater show on our date, or we did just about anything you could think of in New York, often spending time with others. One Sunday, May and Stan Rapport, Vera and I and others were going to go on a hay ride. We had previously bought a portable radio, which I was hooking up in the car on the way to the hay ride. I was putting the antenna on the window, and Vera's brother, who was driving the car, was looking at what I was doing instead of looking where he was driving. He drove the car right into a fire hydrant, the bumper jumping the hydrant. We didn't know what to do, so we went to get Vera's dad who came with a big crowbar. We picked the car up and snapped it off the hydrant. As we left, the hydrant was spurting water up into the air. We went on the hay ride to Echo Lake Park. May was a Bronx New Yorker who had never been in this kind of a place, full of people picnicking. She left to find the bathroom and hadn't returned after an hour. She had gotten lost and was roaming in the park

---

in 1998. In May of 2011, the owners of the Mohegan Sun announced a joint venture with the current owner of the Concord Resort to build a new $600 million dollar resort on the site. The plans are for the new resort to include a 258-room hotel, 75,000-square-foot casino, five restaurants, a harness racing facility and grandstand, and a simulcast facility for pari-mutuel wagering.

and couldn't find us. The dozen of us spread out to go looking for her.

On December 7, 1941, we had gone to the movies in the afternoon to see *Honky Tonk,* a Lana Turner and Clark Gable movie. Since we didn't have a car, we always went locally. After the picture was over, we went back to the store, which was around the corner from where Vera lived. When we walked into the store, everybody was hovered around the radio, and we were told that the Japanese had bombed Pearl Harbor. The following day, President Roosevelt declared war on Japan. After listening to the radio for many hours, Vera and I sat in a corner booth to talk about what we were going to do because it was evident that I would be going into the Army at any time. We decided to get engaged and announced it to her parents. Later that night when I went home to the Bronx, I told my mother and sister about the engagement. Everyone was very happy. Vera was very well liked by my mother, sister and the rest of the family, and I was quite acceptable to her family.

On Monday, December 8th, I went to the Army Air Force offices on Whitehall Street in New York City to enlist as a pilot. I was given a physical and rejected due to my need for glasses. Over the next two days, I tried to enlist as a navigator and bombardier, but was also rejected. After the declaration of war, the various services began to announce all sorts of programs. The Army Signal Corps announced a program that would enable an individual to complete his college education at Swarthmore College in Pennsylvania and simultaneously receive training in Radio Engineering. It was an eight-month session and, upon completion, an enrollee would become a civilian employee of the Signal Corps inspecting aircraft communication systems.

Vera and I decided to marry at the end of the session, on September 21, 1942 in New York City, returning to Philadelphia after a four-day honeymoon. I was assigned to work with a company called Molded Insulation Company, checking and inspecting communication equipment for planes, and Vera got a position with the Director of Personnel. At first we lived with my cousins, Sylvia and Dave Rice, sleeping in a single bed. Then for a few months, we rented a room with kitchen privileges in a private home. About the third month, we were able to get an apartment in a building that had only one-room apartments. The apartment consisted of a fair-sized living room with a Murphy bed[18] in one wall, and a very small kitchen and bathroom. It was furnished with a couch and two armchairs, one of which had to be moved every night in order to take down the bed. The quaint thing about this situation was that on Saturdays we would rent a vacuum cleaner for a quarter from someone in the building to vacuum our bedroom-living room rug. It was a very nice place and the location was within walking distance of the factory where we worked.

The work was very interesting and required talent on how to do things under stress. For example, they had a carton of equipment that needed to be waterproofed in case it fell in the water when it was unloaded from a vessel on its way overseas. The only way I could think to do this was to submerge the carton in a big tub of wax. When the carton was removed, it was completely coated with wax. We then took the box and put it into a tub of water and left it there overnight. The next morning, when we cut the box open, it was perfectly dry. And this was the way things went – there was always something new because nobody had ever done a lot of these things. We weren't in a war before.

In 1943, we continued to reside in our Philadelphia apartment, and since there was no indication of being called to war, Vera became pregnant in October or November of 1943. In April of 1944, I saw an ad in the paper – an Army officer was going overseas, and he had a train set for sale. As a youngster, I always wanted trains, so we decided to buy the train set. It was huge – 7 boxes of Lionel trains and equipment. We stacked the boxes in one corner of our apartment. Everybody would say to me, "How come you bought trains? You don't know if it will be a boy or a girl." I said, "If it's a girl, we'll *teach* her how to play with trains."

---

[18] As the story goes, William Murphy lived in a one-room apartment in San Francisco around 1900 and wanted to invite friends over, including lady friends. Either Mr. Murphy, or his landlady, or just the morals of the time, deemed it scandalous for a woman to be in a man's bedroom. So Murphy, with the help of a blacksmith, designed a bed that could flip into a closet to hide it.

In June, I received notice that I was to be drafted in July. It turned out that the job I had with the Signal Corps was a civilian job, and I was not connected to the Army at all. This was never explained to me when I took the job. Since the baby was due in July, I went to the draft board for a deferment, and I was given until August 1st.

After my father's death, my mother continued as a silent partner in Paul's Lingerie Store on Broadway in New York, which was run by a very dear friend of the family, Paul Volchok. On the day of my son, Ken's, bris, Paul was packing up a gag gift for us when a man came into the store and held him up. Being the type of person that he was, Paul started to push the guy out of the store, and the man shot and killed Paul.

At the time that Paul was shot, technically the store belonged to him. Although there was nothing in writing, the understanding was that he and my mother were partners, and his wife, Anna, had no problem with that. Anna wanted to try running the store, but at the time, I was leaving to go into the service. I again went to the draft board and was given a deferment until September 1st. My mother was in no way going to work in the store, so we decided that Anna should buy us out, and she did. Of course, Uncle Misha was still around, and he helped her out. It took a little while to learn how to take care of customers because she had never worked before, but soon the store was successful. Later, she sold it and moved to Florida.

After straightening out the store issues, I reported for service at Fort Dix, N.J., then shipped to Sheppard Field, Texas, where I went through my basic training. It was a very difficult place to be. In the morning, Texas sand would blow across Sheppard Field to Oklahoma, and in the evening Oklahoma blew back the sand, so we were always eating sand. Plus, the water had a high sulfur content, to the extent that we were using Coca Cola to brush our teeth. After basic training, there was an announcement requesting a bunch of us to report to headquarters with all our gear. Twenty-five of us gathered and were told that we were going to be shipped to Ft. Belvoir, Virginia, for photographic school. It seemed logical – during my days prior to college, I was an amateur photographer and had won many photography prizes. We arrived at Ft. Belvoir via train and were in a large courtyard with about a thousand men. A sergeant came out and directed those in transit school to go here, those in some other training, to go there. Suddenly, everyone's gone but the 25 of us. The sergeant wanted to know why we were there, and the man who had the travel orders said we were there for photography school. The sergeant said there was no photography school there and asked for our travel orders. Sure enough, the orders indicated photography school. He went inside to check, then said there was a typographical error. It should have said phototopography school – they wanted people to make maps from aerial photographs. Three months later, we were phototopographers and reassigned to various reconnaissance squadrons, I to Oklahoma's 41st Air Reconnaissance Squadron. The P-38 airplanes[19], loaded with 3 cameras in the fuselage, and without armament, would fly over a site at a very high speed. One camera was level and the other two were angled on each side of the plane. These three cameras took 25-mile wide photographs.

We left Muskogee, Oklahoma, in March and went to Ft. Lewis in Seattle, Washington, where we waited two weeks before boarding a ship with 5,000 men bound for Hawaii on April 12th, the day Franklin Roosevelt died. This was when I developed a distaste for the Red Cross. When we were in Seattle, we would go to the USO.[20] Although I didn't smoke, there were many men

---

[19]The Lockheed P-38 Lightning was a World War II American fighter aircraft built by Lockheed. The P-38 had distinctive twin booms and a single, central nacelle containing the cockpit and armament. Named "fork-tailed devil" by the Luftwaffe and "two planes, one pilot" by the Japanese, the P-38 was used in a number of roles, including dive bombing, level bombing, ground-attack, photo reconnaissance missions, and extensively as a long-range escort fighter when equipped with drop tanks under its wings. The P-38 was unusually quiet for a fighter, the exhaust muffled by the turbo-superchargers. It was extremely forgiving, and could be mishandled in many ways, but the rate of roll was too slow for it to excel as a dogfighter.[8] The P-38 was the only American fighter aircraft in production throughout American involvement in the war, from Pearl Harbor to Victory over Japan Day.

[20]As it became clear that the nation was heading into World War II, several organizations mobilized to support the growing U.S. military: the Salvation Army, Young Men's Christian Association, Young Women's Christian Association, National Catholic Community Services, National Travelers Aid

who did and they would buy their cigarettes for 10 or 15 cents a pack. They found a label on the bottom that said, "Donated by the Teamsters Union." I didn't like that the Red Cross would sell things that were donated. The other reason for my distaste was that when we were on board the ship to Hawaii, there was a contingent of Red Cross women who were going overseas, and they never left the top deck where the officers were. We felt they should have mingled with the enlisted men also, but they never did. These two incidents made me very anti-Red Cross for many years.

In Hawaii, we were at a small air base on the island of Oahu where the runway crossed the highway. Whenever a plane took off, we had to stop all traffic. We were only there for one month, but during this time they asked for volunteers to create and run a canteen, and I volunteered. My only experience in retail was from my Philadelphia cousin who owned a drug store. When I visited him, I learned some of the retail business. So I ran the canteen in Hawaii, a most delightful place. I had many opportunities to travel around the islands and got to like it very much. After the war, I would have very serious thoughts about moving there.

We left Hawaii and went to Guam[21] where we were told the island had been secured. We had to climb down rope ladders on

---

Association and the National Jewish Welfare Board. President Franklin D. Roosevelt created synergy among these agencies by forming the United Service Organizations (USO), with the objective of providing the emotional support the troops needed.

[21] Guam is in the western Pacific Ocean, the largest and southernmost of the Mariana Islands, and is an organized, unincorporated territory of the United States. The island's capital is Hagåtña (formerly Agaña). The Chamorros, Guam's indigenous people, first populated the island approximately 4,000 years ago and there was a long history of European colonialism. First discovered by Ferdinand Magellan on March 6, 1521, Spain established the first colony in 1668. The island was controlled by Spain until 1898, when it was surrendered to the United States as part of the Treaty of Paris following the Spanish-American War. Guam was captured by the Japanese on December 8, 1941, hours after the bombing of Pearl Harbor, and was occupied for two and a half years. Guam was subject to fierce fighting when US troops recaptured the island on July 21, 1944, a date commemorated every year on Guam as Liberation Day.

the side of the ship into boats which took us to shore. Because of our planes and the runways needed, we had a large base. We were put into two–man tents. The third night that we were there, we were awakened at 4:00 AM by gun shots. They found four Japanese soldiers wearing brand new Army fatigues, and in their pockets they had the latest edition of *Time* and *Readers Digest.* Of course, they were shot. The next night when we heard footsteps, everybody had the same thought, that these were more Japanese soldiers. The safety clips on our rifles came off, and you could hear them being clicked. It turned out that it was the first sergeant notifying the men for KP duty. That morning, all the ammunition from our rifles was removed.

We were very badly needed on Guam because we produced target maps, and so most of our equipment, except for the barracks, dining hall, and kitchens, went unpacked. With another squadron, we were put to work on a round-the-clock basis. The airplanes would go to wherever the assignment was, do the aerial photography, and return, and we would make maps from the photographs. I even worked on the Hiroshima and Nagasaki[22] maps. At the time we worked on them, we only knew the city and that it was going to be bombed, but we never knew what kind of bomb or any details. Every time our planes flew on a reconnaissance mission, we were considered part of the battle and, as a result, we would get a battle star, 8 total. To us, it was a big joke because here we were sitting in an air-conditioned room working on the maps, and we would get a battle star. Not until the end of the war did we realize there was a significance to the battle stars.

---

[22]The United States had called for a surrender of Japan during World War II in the Potsdam Declaration, which was ignored. By executive order of President Harry S. Truman, the U.S. dropped the nuclear weapon "Little Boy" on the city of Hiroshima on Monday, August 6, 1945, followed by the detonation of "Fat Man" over Nagasaki on August 9. These two events are the only active deployments of nuclear weapons in war. The target of Hiroshima was a city of considerable military importance, containing Japan's Second Army Headquarters, as well as being a communications center and storage depot.

Following the end of the war, our map skills weren't needed so they had to find new jobs for us. My job was taking pictures of the construction sites around the island. I would take a picture of a building and the next week go back and take another so others could compare the progress of the construction. The generals didn't want to go out in the heat – 105 degrees was a cool day. When I went to the motor pool to get someone to drive me, the sergeant told me to drive. When I said I didn't know how he showed me, and in two days I was driving, although I had stripped the gears on three jeeps. I got to see a large part of Guam. The thought occurred to me that there were some very nice scenic views and that ordinarily when you traveled, you would buy scenic postal cards at the store. There was no such thing on Guam, so I got the idea to make a packet of 20 scenic views of the island which I sold to the GIs, Marines, and sailors. I did quite well -- my expenses were zero since I just went to the lab and developed and printed my own pictures.

Around November, plans were made to return us to the States and points were tallied based on various events: 5 for a battle star, 1 for every month in service, 2 for every month overseas, 12 if you were married and had a child. You would be discharged, based on total points, highest going first. Most of us only knew approximately, but not exactly, how many points we had. On December 7, I was called to headquarters with a bunch of other men and given discharge papers because I had a sufficient amount of points. I had some 70 points, which was considered a lot, and the 8 battle stars had given me 40 points of those points. I was delighted.

On December 7th, I shipped out aboard the aircraft carrier, USS Ranger, to Angel Island[23], the sister island to Alcatraz, in

---

[23] In 1905, the War Department transferred 20 acres of land on Angel Island (in the middle of San Francisco Bay) to the Department of Commerce and Labor for the establishment of an immigration station. During World War II, the immigration station's barracks and hospital housed German, Italian and Japanese prisoners of war before they were sent to inland camps. Down the shore, Fort McDowell was used as a port of embarkation during both world wars, shipping more than 300,000 soldiers to the Pacific Theater during World War II. The post's busiest period was at the end of the war, when 23,632 returning soldiers were processed in December 1945 alone. The army

San Francisco Harbor. I was taken to an air base in Sacramento, then shipped to Ft. Dix where I was discharged on January 1, 1946.

Upon returning, I was all for the idea of going to Hawaii. I thought it would be the up and coming place. After giving it serious thought, Vera and I concluded that it wouldn't be feasible. At that time, it took almost three weeks to get to Hawaii and the cost was high. We had only Ken at that point, but we considered that the families wouldn't be able to see the children and the children wouldn't see their grandparents. There was Vera's mother, father, brother and sister, and I had a mother and sister, so Hawaii was out of the question. We didn't visit Hawaii until 1982, forty years later, when getting there was only a matter of hours, not weeks. It was a very interesting place, and we probably would have done very well.

An aside on my sister, Rubia:

I never discovered who I was named after. It had to be somebody in the generation before my grandfather's, but my sister, Rubia, born on July 9, 1925, was named after my grandfather, Reuben, who had died in 1924. Rubia married Robert Kaplan on June 19, 1944, at 12:00 in the afternoon. Bob had just finished his Air Force training and was going to be shipped overseas any day, so they decided to get married in New York. Bob's father wanted them to be married by a town official. With difficulty, we were able to arrange it, but when we got to City Hall on the day of the wedding something had come up and the Mayor had left. We were in a bind, so we called the rabbi who had married Vera and me. He was very kind and said to come over and he would perform the ceremony. From the chapel, we went to a Russian restaurant for a wedding dinner. Two weeks after the wedding, Bob shipped out to England as a radio gunner

---

decommissioned the island in 1946, but returned in the 1950s when a Nike missile base was constructed. This was decommissioned as obsolete in 1962. Today, the Angel Island U.S. Immigration Station has been designated a National Historic Landmark.

with the Eighth Air Force on a B-17[24]. When Ken was born July 10th, we sent Bob a special delivery letter about Ken's arrival. It took 6 weeks for that letter to arrive.

Bob flew many missions. On one of his missions, the pilot was killed and the co-pilot was injured. Bob had unsuccessfully gone through pilot training, so was made a radio gunner, but because he remembered his pilot training, he was able to bring the plane back to England. On another one of his missions, his plane was shot down in France. According to protocol, the crew divided up into pairs. Bob and his buddy went their way, working their way to the coast in France where they found French resistance fighters and a ship that took Bob and his buddy back to England. He later received appropriate medals.

Bob stayed in England for R & R, then returned to Florida where Rubia joined him. They lived in Florida until he was discharged in October, 1945. Rubia and Bob moved to New York to live with my mother who had an apartment in the Bronx. If someone rang the doorbell while Bob was asleep, he would wake and look for an escape hatch, trying to jump out the window, because a sound like a doorbell was the signal to abandon his plane. My sister convinced him to go to the Veterans Administration where he was given treatments that enabled him to overcome the situation.

Bob had gone into the service at the age of 18, so when he was discharged he had no trade or profession. My uncle, Misha, suggested to my uncle, Octave, the fur designer, that he take

---

[24] The Boeing B-17 Flying Fortress was a four-engine heavy bomber aircraft developed in the 1930s that was primarily employed by the United States Army Air Forces (USAAF) against German industrial and military targets. The United States Eighth Air Force, based at Thorpe Abbotts airfield in England, participated in Operation Pointblank (the code name for a bomber offensive to impose heavy losses on the German fighter force prior to the Normandy invasion) to help secure air superiority over the cities, factories and battlefields of Western Europe in preparation for Operation Overlord (the code name for the Battle of Normandy on June 6, 1944 , also known as D-Day). The B-17 was a potent, high-flying, long-range bomber that was able to defend itself and return home despite extensive battle damage. It dropped more bombs than any other U.S. aircraft in World War II and was retired in 1968.

Robert into his business and teach him how to be a designer and pattern maker for fur coats. Octave taught Bob all that he could. In 1948, Bob got a job as a designer with a fur shop in Newark, so they bought a house near our house in Hillside. He subsequently got a job with a Chicago company around 1959 that had fur concessions in department stores all over the country, and the family moved to Glenview, Illinois. This company had a policy whereby an individual could only stay in one location for 3 years[25].

Shortly after their 3 years were up in St. Louis, Rubia and Bob moved to a Los Angeles suburb where they resumed relations with our cousin, Ditta, and my Aunt Fannie and Uncle Misha, who had both retired and now lived in California. From Los Angeles, Rubia and Bob moved to a New Orleans suburb and were living on a large lake. They bought a boat and found Louisiana to be a lovely place to live. Once again, the company policy of 3 years came into effect, and they moved to Atlanta, Georgia. There was a highway that went in a circle around Atlanta, with 7 department stores on the highway. Bob was given a position of manager of the 7 stores on this highway, and Rubia worked as a manager for one of the stores. Rubia and Bob liked Georgia and prevailed upon the company not to ship him out at the end of his 3 years. They built a lovely home on stilts on the edge of Lake Lanier.[26] The first floor was very high up and

---

[25]Each year in the spring, Rubia and Bob would come east, staying with Vera and me, so Bob could attend a New York fur stylist trade show. Around this time, I had had difficulties with my Uncle Leo over buying a farm. My sister invited my aunt and uncle to our house without asking me if it was alright. When I told her she should have asked me if it was alright to invite him, she got angry, moved out, and we didn't speak to each other for seven years. We got back together again when my mother became ill in Florida.

[26]Lake Lanier (officially Lake Sidney Lanier) is a reservoir in the northern portion of the U.S. state of Georgia. It was created by the completion of Buford Dam on the Chattahoochee River in 1956, and is also fed by the waters of the Chestatee River. It was named for poet Sidney Lanier, born in 1842, and was built and is operated by the U.S. Army Corps of Engineers (USACE). The USACE is a federal agency and a major Army command made up of civilian and military personnel to comprise the world's largest public engineering, design and construction management agency. Although generally associated with dams, canals and flood protection in the United States, USACE is

underneath was a garage and a tremendous rec room. They were there 2 or 3 years when Bob had a stroke (around 1985) and was paralyzed on his right side. He was using a mechanized wheel chair, like a scooter, and was able to get around well. The problem was that the first floor was high up and there was no way of getting up and down those stairs with a wheelchair. After some serious computations, Bob's son-in-law, Steve, built a ramp from the house's deck to the ground level, figuring that for every inch of height he had to go six feet out. Unfortunately, part of the land between the house and the water belonged to the Corps of Engineers, and the ramp had to be built over 10 feet of the Corps' land. After Steve built the ramp, the Corps told him to remove it, but if they removed it, there would be no way for Bob to get in and out of the house. So Rubia's second daughter, Bonnie, explained the situation to one of the reporters at a local news station, and the story appeared on their program. The response by the public was so great that the Corps of Engineers rescinded the order to remove the ramp. A year ago, Bob and Rubia decided to move. When they went to sell the house, the Corps said the ramp had to come down since it was only for Robert's convenience. Bob and Rubia now live in a house that is all on one level, so he can get around. They celebrated their 65th wedding anniversary in 2009[27].

After I returned from the war, Vera became pregnant and the baby was due in June. We thought maybe we ought to live on a farm since Leo and Bella had bought a farm in the early '40s, and we liked it very much. We rented a little made-over garage with a 4-room apartment, and I worked at the feed mill cooperative run by the farmers while we looked to buy a farm. Every time we found one that seemed good, my uncle said the price was too high. He, of course, was comparing prices to when he started out and bought 40 acres of land with a house and a barn for $3,000. Now houses like that were selling for $30,000 - $40,000. Unfortunately, Vera miscarried. Vera's Dad came down and said, "If you guys don't pack up and move to Newark, I'm going to

---

involved in a wide range of public works support to the nation and the Department of Defense throughout the world.

[27] Rubia passed away on June 25, 2011.

shoot the both of you." After much thought, we moved back to Newark.

I started work at Wilner's Liquor Store as a manager of one of their stores, and we lived with my in-laws. My father-in-law came home one day and said he had found the perfect house in Hillside for us. It looked great from the outside and had a living room, dining room, kitchen, and big hall downstairs, three bedrooms on the second floor, and an attic. There was a tenant in the building, so we couldn't get in to see the interior, but my father-in-law said he had been looking through the windows when the tenant wasn't around and it was a very nice house. We bought it for $8,400[28] and, after four months, we were able to take title to it in May. When we went into the house, we were so upset. The heating system was a big grate on the floor of the hall where the heat from the furnace came up. There were no radiators. If you went into the bathroom and closed the door, you froze your behind off. There were pull chain lights, and it was just a horror. We put the house up for sale immediately, and for three weeks we didn't get a single offer. People looked at it, but nobody wanted to buy it. We decided to stay and remodel the house. We put in a brand new Youngstown[29] metal kitchen, oil heat, changed the electric to switches, and spent $4,000 to modernize the house. We moved in June 1st and had the house livable when Eileen was born on June 28, 1947. The house ended up being a doll house, and we lived there for five years.

In the meantime, my in-laws had bought a building in the Ivy Hill section of Newark which was near a large residential development project. They were building 4-family houses, two 2-family houses together with an owner in one apartment and a tenant in the second, which were sold to GIs and others. My father-in-law pointed out that there were no hardware stores in the neighborhood and that this would be a good place for one. My in-laws had always been in the retail business in one way or

---

[28] Average prices in 1947: car $1,500; gas 23 cents/gallon; house $13,000; bread 12 cents/loaf; postage stamp 3 cents; stock market 181; average annual salary $3,500.

[29] Youngstown Kitchens were the #1 brand of steel kitchen cabinets across America in the postwar period.

another, so they knew a lot about retailing. The building they bought had seven stores, and Vera and I took one over and opened Mount Vernon Variety Store, a hardware/housewares store, in September, 1947.

When we opened the store, it was rather difficult since our income was very low. Fortunately, the Army had a 52/20 club where you got $20/week for 52 weeks, and there were other GI benefits to which we were entitled, like a mortgage rate of 4-1/2% and mortgage insurance. I had a bad knee, so because of that I got medical benefits. Also, at that time, taxes were very low, only $240 a year on the house.

People started coming in asking if I knew anyone who could do repairs. Many of them I could do, so I would close the store from 11:30 AM to 1:00 PM to install chains in windows or attach a clothesline to a pole. When Eileen was 3 years old and Ken was in kindergarten, Vera went to work in the store so we didn't have to close it for me to do the repairs. When we first opened the store, I would come home at night, grab something to eat and then go to work in a leather factory from 7 PM – 12 AM making wallets to supplement our income. After a while, that became difficult. Reading the papers, I discovered an ad from an insurance company that wanted people to do inspections. Unknown to people then, when they took out automobile insurance, an inspector secretly looked the car over and talked to the neighbors to find out what sort of driver the insured was. I did this job during the daytime for three years while Vera was in the store.

In 1950, the construction of the 4-family houses in the area had ground to a halt and the builder started to build 2 one-families together, which didn't sell well. The tract of land he was building on was the former grounds of the Shade Tree Bureau of Newark, and it was very large. He came up with the idea of building 5 apartment buildings, 500 apartments in each building. We immediately saw that the neighborhood would change and that a hardware/houseware/paint store would not be needed, but a general store would be. Our store was 16' x 50', and we knew this would not be adequate, so we extended the store in back by another 32' x 50', making it a 2,400 square foot store. We changed it to a general 5 & 10, and we sold sewing notions, greeting cards, and everything and anything you could think of.

We decided to sell items that were not readily available in the Kings Supermarket which was across the street and or in the stores that were opening up, such as Two Guys from Harrison, and Korvettes, and we looked for merchandise that was unusual and which would be wanted by the neighborhood people. Merchandise was priced so that people would stay in the neighborhood to shop. We found that the big stores usually sold their $2 items for $1.50 – $1.75. Since it wasn't worth the time, gasoline or small savings for someone to drive to the highway, we decided to sell only toys lower than $10, and this gave us a good edge. We also realized that the population of the big apartment buildings in the area was mostly newcomers to America who tended to be homemakers who made their own clothes. So we went into the fabric business, completely stocking a sewing section in our store. We had a total inventory of 9,000 buttons. Vera taught knitting and needlepoint, and I moved into the business of picture framing which worked well with the needlepoint because we were able to offer a complementary service.

Our greeting cards went exceptionally well. We got a printing press and offered to imprint cards free of charge if the customer bought a ten dollar box of cards. At Christmas time, we sent out letters to doctors, lawyers, dentists, all kinds of professionals, offering this service. One memory I have is of a young man who was delivering newspapers to the two apartment houses in the area, which meant there was a possibility of delivering 1,000 newspapers a day. Of course, he didn't have that many, but he delivered quite a number of papers, so we made a deal with him. If he bought his greeting cards from us, we would imprint the cards free of charge because of the quantity. The store started to do very well, and we gradually hired additional people, 6 in all.

We supplemented the store income with other businesses. Some on our own, some with others. My father-in-law, Louis Lipman, was very innovative. He had a large pet shop and horsemeat butcher store, and he would sell his horsemeat to bologna factories which used it as beef. (They knew it was horsemeat.) He also had a beef bologna factory customer in downtown Newark. For a long time, twice a week at 6:00 in the morning, I would deliver a 500-pound barrel of horsemeat.

By 1952, Eileen was in kindergarten and Ken was in the third grade, and we found a four-family house on Ellery Avenue which backed up to the Ivy Street School playground. At that time, it was a grammar school. The house had two five-room apartments on the second floor and two four-room apartments on the first floor. We took one bedroom from one of the five-room apartments, closed off the door, then cut a door into our side to give us a six-room, three-bedroom apartment. It was quite nice and within walking distance of the store and school. At the same time, my mother-in-law and father-in-law and my sister-in-law and her family built and moved into a house a block away from the store.

Eileen was very good with children and, even though she was only 6 years old, after school she would walk to my in-laws' house and play and take care of my sister-in-law's baby who was only about a year old at the time. Shortly thereafter, because of the thousand tenants in the apartment houses, the builder built a school. Called the Mt. Vernon School, it was five blocks from the store. We started selling large amounts of school supplies because we had Ivy School, now a junior high school, and Mt. Vernon School, up to the sixth grade, in the area, and the children from the apartment houses had to pass our store every day on the way to the junior high school.

I had no liking for my father-in-law. Every Friday morning before we would open our store, either Vera or I would go to her parents' store to write their checks, make deposits, keep the books, etc. One Friday morning, Vera went but didn't show up at our store at her usual 10:00 time. I called my mother-in-law who thought Vera went home. When I called the house and Vera answered, I could tell from her voice that something wasn't right. She had gotten into an argument with her father after he had hit my mother-in-law and told her to get out of the store. Vera was quite upset for about 5 days until we made the decision to avoid contact with her father. When we went to her parents' store, we demanded that he not be there, otherwise we were not coming, and we didn't go to their house to visit either. They needed us to do their books so her father had to comply with the demand that he not be in the store.

This, of course, was upsetting to Vera, but she and her mother would see each other on Thursday mornings when they went to the beauty parlor together. I didn't see my mother-in-law that often, but it was more important that Vera saw her. It was a very stressful time. Pop, my father-in-law, just wasn't a nice person. We couldn't completely disengage with him because he would come up with these ideas that he wanted me to develop. To avoid conflicts, I would do it. He treated me nicely because he needed me. Moving to Maplewood helped the situation by distancing us from him.

My father-in-law would often go to Laurel Gardens[30] on Springfield Avenue in Newark. Pop would go see Lou Halper[31], one of his friends, box, and other friends wrestle. Pop was a gambler of the nth degree. He played cards constantly. In fact, he once had a particularly disastrous card game. When Vera was around ten or eleven years old, Pop walked in and said to my mother-in-law, "Pack up, we're leaving." When she asked what he meant, he told her he had lost the store. He gambled on everything, even on things he didn't know much about—

---

[30] Laurel Garden was originally operated as a German beer garden and showhouse for German films. Sometime in the 1920s, it was purchased by Charlie Zemel whose formal education ended when he was expelled from the sixth grade in a school in Newark's Ironbound section. The arena was used for many things – boxing on Mondays and wrestling on Thursdays. Some of the biggest names in boxing fought here, including Max Schmeling and James Braddock. On nights when there was no boxing or wrestling, it was used as a roller skating rink. Although the building was demolished in 1953, Zemel owned the property until his death in 1980 at the age of 104. He also owned hundreds of other Newark properties, including more than 1,000 rental units, the Newark Armory, and three theatres.

[31] Lou Halper, 1909 – 1973, got his start as a boxer at Laurel Garden. He hawked newspapers outside on boxing nights, later moving inside as a fighter when he figured out he could make more money inside in the ring. As a professional, Halper fought in every division from flyweight to middleweight and was ranked as the number 10 middleweight in the world for January and February 1935 by Ring magazine. He was inducted into the New Jersey Boxing Hall of Fame.

basketball, hockey, football. The only thing he knew about was baseball, and he bet on all the games.

At one time, when prohibition ended in 1932 or 1933, Pop had a tavern and Longie Zwillman[32], a wheeler dealer that Pop hung around with, told him he had to sell Potts beer on the fountain. There were barrels and barrels of Potts Beer in the cellar, but the spigots on the fountain in the tavern showed Ballantine[33] and

---

[32] Abner "Longie" Zwillman (July 27, 1904 - February 27, 1959), a Prohibition gangster, was known as the "Al Capone of New Jersey." After his father died in 1918, he quit school to support his family, selling produce in his neighborhood with a rented horse and wagon. Unable to compete with the pushcarts, he moved to the better Clinton Hill neighborhood where he sold lottery tickets to local housewives. He found that he could make much more money selling lottery tickets than produce so concentrated on selling lottery tickets through local merchants and, with the help of hired muscle, by 1920 he controlled the bulk of the numbers racket. During Prohibition, Zwillman smuggled whiskey through Canada into New Jersey, expanding into illegal gambling, prostitution, and racketeering, as well as legitimate businesses, including several prominent night clubs and restaurants. By the late 1920s, Zwillman had an estimated income of $2 million per year. He dated actress Jean Harlow and got her a two-picture deal at Columbia Pictures by giving its head, Harry Cohn, a huge loan. He later married Mary Mendels, the only daughter of Eugene Mendels, a founder of the American Stock Exchange. Zwillman often sought to legitimize his image, offering a reward for the return of the Lindbergh baby in 1932, and contributing to charities, including $250,000 to a Newark slum-clearing project. He was involved in local politics, eventually controlling many Newark politicians for over twenty years and dominating gambling operations in New Jersey. Zwillman was issued a subpoena to testify during the 1959 McClellan Senate Committee hearings on organized crime, but shortly before he was to appear, Zwillman was found hanged in West Orange, New Jersey. Although his death was ruled a suicide because of his income tax problems, police found bruises on his wrists, supporting the theory that Zwillman had been tied up before being hanged. It's often speculated that either Vito Genovese or Meyer Lansky had ordered Zwillman killed.

[33] The Ballantine Company, originally the Patterson & Ballantine Brewing Company, was founded in 1840 in Newark, New Jersey, by Peter Ballantine (1791–1883), from Scotland. In the 1850s, Ballantine bought out his partner, his three sons joined the business, and he renamed the company P. Ballantine and Sons, which would be used until the company closed its brewery in 1972. By 1879, it had become sixth largest brewery in the US, almost twice as large as Anheuser-Busch. Since 2005, the Ballantine Ale brand has been owned and

Krueger[34] beer. When someone asked for a Ballantine beer, they got a glass of Potts beer. One day, four men came in and sat down at a table and ordered four Krueger beers. Pop brought over four beers. The men drank it and one of them said, "This isn't Krueger beer. I'm Krueger." Two of the men with him were from the Division of Alcoholic Beverage Control, and they closed up the tavern – forever. Afterwards, Longie Zwillman gave Pop a lot of money, and he went into the candy store business. Many years later Zwillman was found hanging in his basement. They never knew whether he was murdered or committed suicide.

Pop came up with the idea of bird ornaments and parakeet[35] toys, and we started the L & B Novelty Company (Louis and Bernie). We called the ornament, The Happy Birdie. Our item consisted of a metal cut-out like a parakeet, and below it was a mirror with a perch coming out of the bottom. The parakeet is a love bird, and when a bird sat on the perch and looked in the mirror, it saw another bird and it would coo and make love to the bird. This item was patented in Washington, and we sold it for about ten years, mostly via mail order to the stores, never retail.

In the 1950s, it was quite a fad to close a room's windows and doors, open the cage and let the bird fly around. We made large wheels, step ladders, all kind of toys out of quarter-inch diameter plastic tubing. Of course, whenever Pop had an idea, it was given

---

marketed by the Pabst Brewing Company, which outsources the brewing to the Miller Brewing Company.

[34]The Gottfried Krueger Brewing Company was a brewery in Newark, New Jersey, founded by Gottfried Krueger and John Laible (Gottfried's Uncle) in 1858.The company produced Krueger Beer, the first beer to be produced in cans, in 1935. The brewery was ultimately purchased by Ballantine and Sons.

[35]Parakeets have been very popular due to their striking coloring, cheerful nature, small size, and their affordability. Originally from Australia, the parakeet in the wild flies in huge flocks consisting of thousands of birds. They are very social with lots of personality. As youngsters, the male and female look similar, however as a male matures, his nostrils will become distinctly blue and he may have a blue tint to his legs. The mature female will have pink or flesh colored nostrils and pale pink legs. Parakeets love to chatter and can learn to say several words. Their lifespan is 15 – 20 years.

to me to carry out. So I found places to manufacture the toys, and we very rapidly went into the mail order business, sending our circulars to pet shops all over the East Coast and, later, all over the United States.

The fad only lasted about a year before the birds were kept in the cages, and unfortunately our toys were meant for outside the cage. Some of the bird supply manufacturers went to China and Taiwan and came back with miniatures of the toys we had, which would fit into the cages. We suddenly found ourselves with 60,000 pieces of quarter-inch plastic tubing, 6' long.

Around 1957, hula hoops[36] were the rage. Since they were 3' in diameter, they were too large for the little kids to handle. We created a factory in our basement, and Vera, Eileen, Ken and I worked at night cutting 1" pegs from ¼" dowel rods which we would stick into both ends of a length of plastic tubing, creating a 2' hoop, exactly what youngsters needed. Within 6 months, we had sold our 60,000 pieces of plastic that were left over from the bird toy business.

One of our other enterprises involved making a square rack, 2' on all four sides and 6' tall, and filling this rack with needles, threads, zippers, anything pertaining to sewing. The plan was to have someone build the racks, and I would place them in supermarkets. Around 1962, when I was 43 years old, I took a model to the A&P headquarters in New York City. They put me in a little room where I set up my display. The buyer, a man who looked old enough to be my grandfather, came in. After my explanation, he said, "Sonny, you have a wonderful idea here, but don't put it in the A&P. I like you, so what I'm about to tell you is not according to Hoyle[37]. This will go over very big in the

---

[36]Richard Knerr and Arthur Melin of Wham-O, a California toy company, manufactured a plastic hoop in bright colors that would be whirled around the waist/hip area for play or exercise. More than 100 million hula hoops were sold in the first 12 months on the market.

[37]Meaning, by the rules and attributable to Edmond Hoyle (1672-1769), the English barrister and writer who was the author of several works on card-games. He is cited as the final authority when disputes on the rules of card games arose.

A&P, and you might have 20 or 30 stores for your racks, but then they'll decide to take the idea for themselves. My advice is to put your racks in a smaller supermarket." So I went to the Shop Rite in New Jersey and placed my racks in about 20 stores. Each day, I would go early in the morning to certain stores and service them, at least once a week to each store. I would replenish the merchandise that was sold, bill the store and get the money at what was called 10 EOM (end of the month). After the first year, they notified me that they were now going to pay 10 days at the end of the second month, which meant 60 days before payment. I wasn't happy with that, but I went along with it. In another couple of months, they decided it was to be 3 months, 90 days. I sold off the racks and the merchandise to each store and said goodbye.

In the meantime, I had placed sewing supply racks in 7 drug stores as well as the Newark Slip Company in Newark, and this relationship went on for about 20 years until I went out of business in 1982 and sold the racks to the individual stores.

Around 1960, Vera came up with the idea of a recipe holder that could be put on the counter to keep recipes from being soiled. It was an easel with a bulldog clip on the top. We were able to locate an easel from a company that would add the bulldog clip, so we had 5,000 made up and called them Recipe Caddies. We advertised through a Midwest mail order company where we placed an ad with a coupon on the other side that could be mailed in. Whenever someone ordered a caddy, we had to pay the company 50 cents. Whenever we got an order, we kept the address of the person who ordered. After a while, this grew to quite an active business, and we had another 5,000 recipe caddies manufactured. We decided to have our own mail order catalog, sending them out twice a year, using the names of those who had ordered caddies previously. We had a lot of repeat orders on the caddy plus other catalog items, one of which was a collection of miniature mirrors. When I made picture frames for needlepoint, there were always pieces of molding left over. I would take these pieces and make tiny mirrors out of them, all different shapes and sizes, and these also became good sellers. We also advertised about 5 or 6 items which we carried in the store. For example, TV trays that fit into a stand. These were very popular.

Although we were busy all the time, we were always looking for additional sources of income. One of the salesmen who worked for a toy wholesale company said there was a terrific market for toy racks at stores like Quick Chek and 7-Eleven since they had a large number of customers with children. He proposed taking the same rack that we used for the sewing supplies and placing it, stocked with toys, in the stores. The only difference would be that the store would buy the rack instead of our leasing it to them, and we would stock the rack. So the salesman sold and delivered the racks. My job was to make the racks and stock them every two weeks. It was quite a nice business.

Another steady part of our business related to the large apartment houses in the neighborhood of the store. The apartment walls were made of concrete cinderblock with a brick facing on the outside, and people didn't know how to put up venetian blinds or curtain rods. I was able to get permission from the management of the buildings to put signs up near the mailboxes that I installed window treatments. The thing that most people didn't realize was that you just needed a carboloid drill bit, and then it would go in like butter. That was the whole secret behind our ability to make the installation. If the individual bought the items from us, we would charge one installation price, but if the treatments weren't bought from us, the price was a much higher fee. This, of course, encouraged people to come to the store and buy from us. I would do the installations every afternoon, 1:00 – 3:00 PM. In the morning I was in the store, and Vera would come in late. After 3:00, the school kids would come home and we would have a large influx of people so we had to have more people on the spot.

At the same time, one of my buddies from my younger days, Henny Levee, mentioned that the kitchens in the apartment buildings were very narrow and proposed that we sell drop leaf tables that could attach to the wall. I came up with the idea of taking a piece of plywood, about 2-1/2' x 3-1/2', putting formica across the top and edging it with chrome metal. I found a bracket that could be attached both to the wall and to the table top, and it made a perfect drop leaf when you put 2 chairs around it. I would make the table tops, and my friend would sell and install them.

We did a very nice business with this right up to the time we gave up the store.

We had our problems with pilferage. Nothing was more aggravating than to find a card with one or two buttons or snaps missing. Of course, there were other things that were stolen in their entirety, but those we didn't always know about. We solved the problem by taking the items that were not usually found in other stores and raised every item by 9 cents. We were never concerned about pilferage after that because the increased pricing covered any kind of pilferage. This was the easiest way to take care of the problem.

Although the apartments were never completely full, they would get various influxes of nationalities. When the Alaskan pipeline was under construction, men were brought from Columbia to the pipeline to work. Why, I don't know, but the company brought their families to live at the Ivy Hill Apartments, and the men would visit every month for a week. This meant we had a large number of Spanish-speaking people in our store. So Vera and I went to night school and learned to speak Spanish. One day a woman came in who sounded Hispanic to us. When we started to speak Spanish to her, it turned out she was Portuguese. We didn't learn Portuguese. We were always fascinated with the Chinese and Japanese people, Japanese especially. The first time they came in, they had a dictionary and would bow their heads to us, then look in the dictionary for the word they needed. By the end of the second week, they didn't need a dictionary. They were able to speak to us in English. It was a remarkable thing that they were so quick to learn the language. In the 1970s, there was a tremendous influx of Russian Jewish people. With my little Russian and Vera's little Yiddish, we were able to take care of them, so we became an international settlement.

Of course, one of the reasons all these people came in was because of the Post Office. Two mailmen would go to the apartment house each day, one delivering letters, the other, packages. When the recipient wasn't home, the mailman would leave the package in the hallway or, if it was really large, he would take it back to the Post Office and leave a note to go to the Post Office for pick-up. Not only did some of the packages disappear, but it was inconvenient to pick them up at the Post Office because you had to take a bus to get there. I got to know about this situation and went downtown to the post office and asked the Newark Postmaster to give me a contract station. When the mailman delivered to the apartments and people weren't home, he could leave a slip to pick up the package at 82 Mt. Vernon Place, our store. The Postmaster thought this was a terrific idea, and we negotiated a price. Not only did they pay *me*, but in November and December, I was allowed to hire help to supplement the Post Office and, of course, I hired Vera. We placed the Post Office counter at the very back of the store so people who came in had to walk a hundred feet of store to get something from the Post Office. When a mother came in with her child, the mother might buy a 3 cent stamp, but she often ended up with a $1 toy. So our Post Office was called Contract Station #60, beginning around 1955, 56. It was a very big asset because people from all over the world who lived in the Ivy Hill Apartments were coming into our store. We had the contract right up to the very last day the store was open.

Around 1957, a woman came into our store and introduced herself as our son's junior high school teacher. She said that whenever she asked a question, the first hand up was Ken's, and she couldn't always call on him, as it was unfair to the other students. As a result, he was getting bored. She thought we should enroll him in a private school, or he would get into trouble. Turns out he was an exceptional student. Although he got A's all the time, we hadn't given it much thought. At the time, there was Newark Academy and one or two other private schools, but the tuition was extremely high. Vera and I decided to move from our 6-room apartment in the 4-family house in Newark to a private house in Maplewood or South Orange because Columbia High School was an excellent school. The 3 other apartments in our 4-family house already covered the cost of the property tax and our share of the mortgage, so the income from renting our former apartment plus the money we would save on private tuition would take care of the new mortgage on the house. When we went to a realtor, we drew a circle on a map with the store in the center, telling him that we wanted to be able to walk to the store if necessary. In 3 months, we found a house and moved in during the summer of 1957. It was 3 bedrooms, actually 4. One for Vera and me, one for Ken, one for Eileen, with a bathroom on the second floor and a complete bedroom on the third floor. The house had been owned by the builder of the neighborhood houses who had built himself a larger house with a 3 car garage that had a loft in it. The house had all the piping and everything in the attic to make a bathroom, but we never added one. It was a very beautiful home, large. We had a sun parlor, an enclosed porch, and a beautiful operating fireplace, although we converted it to gas. When Ken went away to college, we converted his bedroom into a sitting room with a sleeping couch and a TV. Years later, this was where our grandchildren would battle when they slept overnight. Everybody wanted the room with the TV. We lived there until 1995.

The neighbor next door to us, Mabel, was a 90-year-old woman, never married, who had worked at the town hall in charge of the welfare department. She was a bigoted woman. I always thought she never knew anybody who was Jewish. We quickly befriended her, because that's our nature. We liked to be friends with everybody. In no time at all, we were taking care of her. Sometimes we would shop for her, and we had an arrangement that she would call us every day at 11:00 AM at the store to tell us if she was well, or not.

A little after we moved in, one of the houses was bought by a black couple. They were lovely people. He was an engineer at Picatinny Arsenal; she was a school teacher in a different town. I thought Mabel would have a heart attack over this, but we were finally able to calm her down.

The snowfalls at that time were rather large, and so I decided to buy a snow blower. Mabel offered to pay half if I would do her driveway and sidewalk, which I did. Strangely enough, one of the things I would do when it snowed was walk down the block – there were only four houses on each side – and blow the snow off the sidewalks. Out of the eight people I did this for, the only people who ever came and thanked me and gave me a bottle of wine for Christmas was the black couple.

We would have family picnics in our backyard because we had a 3-car garage with a very large driveway. The highlight of every picnic was to line up the children according to height.

There were generally around 15 children in line, and we would take pictures so we would know who was there. It wasn't a question of who was there as an adult. It was more important about who was there as a child. We had two children, my sister had four daughters, my cousin, Vicki, had five daughters. One of my buddies would come with his two children and occasionally another very good friend came with his five children. It was always like a three-ring circus. The family stayed together all through the years. The day always ended the same way. My cousin, Vicki, would be in the house saying goodbye. Victor, her husband, was in the car with the five girls bouncing up and down, almost battling with each other, but Vicki took her time to say goodbye to everybody.

I wasn't religious in the formal sense of the word. My father had been persecuted for being Jewish in Russia,[38] so when he came to America he decided not to formally observe the Jewish religion. He didn't join a shul (Orthodox), synagogue (Conservative), or temple (Reform), but he did observe the holidays at home. For example, on Passover we had a Seder. On Rosh Hashana and Yom Kippur, he didn't work and Rubia and I didn't go to school, spending the day together. Beginning when Rubia was five and I was ten, my father would sit us down every month and explain different things about Judaism – its history and customs -- so we were well versed in our religion. My father's feeling was that if you were a good person, you were a good Jew. In later years, I followed his lead. We closed the store on holidays, and we didn't go to religious services until Ken was eight years old, when he started Hebrew school. Since we were at the store on Saturdays, we went every Friday night to services at the Beth David Jewish Center until the children finished their religious training.

We became friends with about thirty families who were members of the Congregation. Among these families, there were four with whom we became very close: Pat and Anita Felber; Mildred and Bob Putman (Bob was Anita's brother); Alex and

---

[38] When my father and his brother, Leo, were growing up, their father would flip a ruble on a page of the Torah. If Kolia or Leo could recite what was under the ruble, he would get it.

Sylvia Goldberg; and Bernice and Mel Jacobs. Once a month, the five couples would get together to play Canasta or Gin Rummy, each time putting money into a kitty. Periodically, we would use the accumulated money to go to dinner and the theater in New York. We spent many other occasions together, including most of the holidays. Once again at Hanukkah, names were pulled out of a bag to buy a single present—to buy for everybody was impossible[39].

When Pat Felber passed away in the late 60s, Anita came to work at the store. On at least two occasions, the children lived with us while Anita recuperated, once from an auto accident, another time from an operation. When Bob Putman passed away in the early 60s, Mildred, Anita, Vera and I would go to the movies and do many things together. Years later, Anita married Phil Lerman and the association continued. It wasn't until 1967 that Anita decided to take a position in an office. The only people left today from the entire group of thirty couples are Anita Lerman (previously Felber), Mildred Putman, Bernice Jacobs and me.

When we moved to Maplewood, we changed our temple because the daughters of our friends were going to the Oheb Shalom synagogue for Hebrew class, and it would be easier for Eileen to go there. Oheb Shalom had a different policy than some temples about bat mitzvahs. They taught the usual things, but they didn't have a formal Torah reading for each girl as they became thirteen. Rather, the temple would conduct a confirmation service in June for all the girls who turned thirteen during the past year, and so Eileen's work was recognized this way with various members of the family attending.

Another family remembrance I have is the Passover Seders[40]. We always celebrated them, although we were not very religious or very observant. One of the families attending always broke the

---

[39] The Felbers had four children, the Putmans, three, the Jacobses, two, and the Goldbergs, one.

[40] The Passover Seder is a Jewish ritual feast that marks the beginning of Passover. It is conducted on the evenings of the 14th day of Nisan in the Hebrew calendar, and on the 15th by traditionally observant Jews living outside Israel, or late March or April in the Gregorian calendar.

fast for Yom Kippur with a dinner, and the location alternated so that everybody hosted at one time or another.

The preliminary and standard part of a Seder is to read the Haggadah[41]. There would be three matzahs[42] on the table. The one who conducted the service would take a matzah, break it up, and pass it around. He would break another in half and hide it. Then the children would look for the matzahs, and the one who found it would get a prize. The children turned the house upside down looking for it. It was always great fun. We would usually end up giving everyone a prize so there was no favoritism.

Family and friends would get together before Hanukkah[43], usually in December, and draw a slip of paper from a bowl to determine for whom they would buy a gift, since it would have been too costly to buy everyone a gift. The night of the Hanukkah party, everyone brought their gift and we would open them according to age, the oldest person first, down to the youngest since, if you gave the youngest his gift right away, he would want to go off and play. All the other holidays were observed with a dinner. Whoever made the dinner would invite whomever they wanted.

Vera often would make a Russian borscht with beets and cabbage. She was very fortunate because she had two people teaching her how to cook. Her mother was the world's worst cook, but my mother and my Aunt Bella were fantastic cooks

---

[41] The Haggadah contains the story of the Israelite exodus from slavery in Egypt, special blessings and rituals, commentaries from the Talmud, and special Passover songs.

[42] Matzah (also Matzoh, Matzo, Matza), an unleavened bread, is the "official" food of Passover. When the Jews were leaving Egypt, there was no time for the bread to rise, and the result was matzah. The ingredients for matzah are flour and water.

[43] Hanukkah, also known as the Festival of Lights, is an eight-day Jewish holiday commemorating the rededication of the Holy Temple (the Second Temple) in Jerusalem. Hanukkah is observed for eight nights and days, starting on the 25th day of Kislev according to the Hebrew calendar, which may occur at any time from late November to late December in the Gregorian calendar. The festival is observed by lighting the nine-branched Menorah or Hanukah, one additional light on each night of the holiday, progressing to eight on the final night.

who taught Vera how to cook and bake. One of Vera's greatest dishes was strudel. People would ask her for her recipe, then make it, and no matter who it was, they never made it as good as hers. She also made gefilte fish[44]. My mother taught her, and there was a dispute. My mother liked to make the fish from four fish: white fish, pike, carp, and buffel, which made the fish look dark. Vera wanted her fish to look white, so she eliminated the buffel and made it with three fish. I liked the four fish, and so Vera would make both kinds. Then we had kugel. It was made from farfel[45], actually crushed matzahs. Farfel from the store could be expensive, but you accomplished the same thing by taking matzahs and crushing them with a rolling pin. Vera made the farfel that way, then added sugar and crushed pineapple and baked it. It was the most delicious kugel you ever tasted. Her potato pancakes and her blintzes were both outstanding. There are so many dishes she made well that it's difficult to enumerate.

We had a family circle which would periodically meet. This family circle was not the Verosub/Golostupitz family, but rather it was Vera's family, the Resnick family. The unusual part of these get-togethers was that everybody who attended owned a store except one person. (Vera's sister was hard of hearing and so was her husband, so her husband worked in a jewelry factory where he was a polisher of gold rings.) We would have discussions about business, where and how to buy goods, etc. At one of these meetings, I recommended that we form a co-op so

---

[44] When the Jews migrated to Eastern Europe, fresh fish was hard to come by. Since nearly all the Jews were extremely poor, they learned to invent inexpensive dishes, with fresh fish being reserved for the Sabbath. Living near the North Sea, they could use pike, carp, buffel, or other inexpensive freshwater fish which spoiled quickly. A fish stretcher—gefilte fish—was concocted so that everyone could have a small taste for the Friday meal. The women scraped the flesh away from the skin and bone, added chopped onions, seasoning, bread or matzah crumbs and egg. The fish was then put back into the skin and poached.

[45] Farfel is a small pellet-shaped pasta made from an egg noodle dough. During Passover, when dietary laws pertaining to grains are observed, matzah farfel takes the place of the egg noodle version.

My Life 59

we could take advantage of volume buying from the manufacturers. One uncle had 17 drug stores, another had 3, an aunt and uncle had a 5 & 10 in Kearny, and Vera and I had our store. The uncle with 17 stores refused to become part of the co-op since he was afraid he would lose the volume discounts he already had, even though I told him he might get greater discounts in the co-op. No amount of talking would convince him to become a member of the co-op, so we never formed one. While the Verosub/Golostupitz family didn't have an actual family circle, we did get together quite regularly and have good times.

Every year, from 1957 on, Vera and I went on vacation by ourselves, first while the kids were at camp and then while they were at college, and we visited almost every country in Europe, except Germany and Austria, and much of the Orient. We would also look for places to vacation that would be of interest to the children first, and to us second. One of our first trips as a family was to Williamsburg, Virginia, over Lincoln's Birthday, and that was a rude awakening. I always knew there was a difference between the northern and southern parts of the United States, but while in Williamsburg, we realized it even more. Lincoln's Birthday was on a Monday -- at that time, the holiday was observed on the actual day -- however because we were in Virginia, one of the states of the Confederacy, all the businesses, banks, and local stores were open. They didn't observe Lincoln's birthday. The only thing in town that wasn't open was the Post Office, a Federal operation. After Williamsburg, we visited Mt. Vernon, Washington's home, and then Monticello, Jefferson's home.

Another trip was to Lancaster, Pennsylvania, in Amish country. This was an exceptional trip. We didn't join a tour group, but we watched where they went and then followed them. The Amish people were very receptive to talking to people who didn't simply focus on the differences between the Amish way of life and the rest of the United States. We learned, for example, that some of them had locked barns. I couldn't understand why, but in our conversations we found that many of them had modern equipment in the barn, like lathes, jigsaws and drill presses, and in some cases they even had a refrigerator. We were surprised to see a telephone in the barn of one home. The Amish were receptive to talking about their children and how they educated them in their own schools. Some of the Amish were angry with some of the non-Amish population who were taking advantage of them, like the companies that specialized in making Amish-style clothing at a much higher cost than ordinary clothes in the stores. There were many people in need of these clothes, not just Pennsylvania, but in colonies all over the United States. One of the interesting people we met was a man who made furniture. His biggest item was small chairs for children. This man had only three fingers on each hand, the two middle fingers of each hand being lost to a saw at various times. He made wonderful furniture, and our family still has one of those chairs. It's 50 years old. We made about four trips to the area, and every time we went we came across interesting people and places. We re-visited some of the people, and they would remember us.

One of the longest trips for the four of us was a two-week August camping trip to Burlington, Vermont. The camp grounds had a lean-to where we were able to set up our four cots, a fireplace where we did our cooking, and a shower house for bathing and other water needs. We visited the Killington Ski Resort, which was just being constructed and took the lift, which had already been built, to the top of the mountain. We visited a quarry and foundry where we saw them excavating the huge slabs of marble, then cutting and polishing them to size. Then there was a sculpture studio, a restored village, and the Shelbourne Museum with the side-paddlewheel steamboat Ticonderoga, which used to sail on Lake Champlain. We explored the entire area for two weeks. On our way home, catastrophe struck when we got a flat. The station wagon was packed to the top with our belongings, and we had to unload the entire back end of the station wagon to get to the spare tire. Despite the flat, it was a wonderful trip.

All through the years, we would go to New York to visit the museums, the two zoos (one in Central Park, one in the Bronx), and many of the well-known churches, like St. Patrick's Cathedral. We always found something new and interesting to do. On one of our New York trips, I was reminiscing about

My Life   61

visiting Theodore Roosevelt's home[46] in downtown New York as a grammar school student. I knew the house was somewhere in the 20s, but which street exactly, I couldn't remember. We stopped to ask a policeman for directions, and he looked at us like we were from another planet. He had never heard of the Roosevelt home and didn't know where it was. We were on a one-way street, so we continued down the street to get out of the area. There in the middle of the block was the Roosevelt home. We stopped to visit it, and they even had all of Roosevelt's athletic equipment from his early years as a frail child, which he used to strengthen his arms and legs.

When I was a youngster, I loved hiking and camping. I was very much interested in being a Boy Scout, however my family felt that the Boy Scouts were a personification of a military organization. At that time, there were the Brownshirts[47] in Germany and the Blackshirts[48] in Italy, and the family felt that the Boy Scouts were similar to that, so I wasn't allowed to join. When my son, Ken, was eight years old in 1952, Vera and I decided that he should have the fun of being a Cub Scout and Boy Scout. I took him to a Cub Scout meeting and walked out as Cub Master. Nobody wanted the position, so I took it. Over the years, I had a great time with the boys. We would sell electric bulbs that came from my store to raise money, then go on a trip. One time, we went to Canada. Then when Ken turned 11, I became his Scout Master. These troops were sponsored by the Beth David Jewish Center and, of course, were mainly made up of young Jewish boys. One day, two Italian boys came to join the

---

[46]Roosevelt was the only U. S. president born in New York City – at 28 East 20th Street – becoming our 26th president.

[47]The Sturmabteilung or SA (in English, Stormtroopers) functioned as a paramilitary organization of the Nazi Party, playing a key role in Adolf Hitler's rise to power. SA men were often called "brownshirts" after the color of their uniforms.

[48]The Blackshirts, officially known as the Voluntary Militia for National Security, were Fascist paramilitary groups in Italy during the period immediately following World War I and until the end of World War II and wore black shirts as part of their uniform.

troop – Daniel and Dominick Mazzagetti – and their mother was anxious for them to become a member of my troop. A year later, she returned to tell me she had a problem, but she didn't care about it. The priest at her church told her to take the boys out of the troop and put them into the scout troop at the church. She told him that I took the boys all over and did lots of things with them, and she wanted her sons to be with me. This presented a problem because every February we would have a Scout night at the Temple when the boys would conduct services, and after services we would have snacks. She wanted to bake, but we couldn't have her bake because her food wasn't kosher, so I had her buy kosher wine in order to satisfy her desire to participate and help.

When Ken and I would go with my Boy Scout troop on a camping trip, Eileen and Vera would stay home and have a marvelous time together. They did things like wash and set their hair, all kinds of girl things, and it was great for them, and it was great for Ken and me.

Fortunately for me, our son was a very studious person and prior to his graduating from high school, he did a thorough job of investigating scholarships for himself.[49] All this information he passed to me, and I in turn would have a session each year in the spring telling my boys what and where to go in order to look for scholarships.[50] The young kids had no idea what scholarships

---

[49] Since Ken had done so well in high school, when he was ready to apply to Harvard, his first choice college, the high school counselor told Ken he wouldn't have any trouble getting in so he needn't apply to other schools. I told Ken, "No way, no how are you applying to one college. Three at minimum." He applied to Michigan, Harvard and Swarthmore, and was put on the waiting list at Harvard, on the waiting list at Swarthmore, and was accepted at Michigan with a scholarship. Ken had five fellowships when he graduated from Michigan, and he had his pick.

[50] I let Ken know how important this information was and how he had helped so many other boys. I later told Ken that he must do the same for his kids. Ellis was a superior student. The Buck family lives in the region of California where Ken lives. The Bucks were the first to ship produce and fruit via refrigerated cars to the East Coast. Mr. Buck became a congressman, and he created ten scholarships a year, based on merit, not need, where the recipient could go to any college he wanted, then continue on to graduate school. They get two trips home a year and a trip to Europe. Ellis got one of those scholarships and went to Harvard.

were available. There was no Internet in those days that would make this research easier. S&H Green Stamps had a scholarship that no one knew about -- $5,000/year. National Newark and Essex Bank had a scholarship. There were dozens of scholarships that weren't known.

As a result of Ken's initial hard work and my sessions with them, many of my scouts were quite successful. One of them came to me and said that his father was a beer truck driver who liked to gamble, and he didn't think he could ever get to college. He wanted to be an electrical engineer. I had a perfect situation for him. The Newark College of Engineering had a scholarship that was created by a young man who went to college there, had been a Boy Scout and had lived in Newark, and those were his criteria for the scholarship. So we went to the Boy Scout office and discovered that no one had applied for this scholarship for seven years. We made the necessary application, and Pat Natel went to Newark College of Engineering and graduated as an electrical engineer. He went on to work for Public Service Electric & Gas Company and is now a Vice President of the company.

Two of my boys, Glen and Jay Jacobs, went to Belgium to medical school, and are today cardiologists. As a result of our troop's monthly Sunday trips to Newark Hospital[51], Bruce Schoenberg developed an interest in medicine. He went to college, got a scholarship at Rutgers, graduated from medical school, became a doctor and subsequently became a member of the United Nations World Health Organization.

Another one of my boys, Lenny Weisman, wanted to go to West Point. I suggested he see his Congressman, which Lenny did, and he was appointed. Lenny told me he wanted to be a doctor afterwards, and I told him he would have to spend five years with the Army after he graduated. I suggested that he talk to someone in the Army to see what they would say, and they said he could go to medical school afterwards. I said get it in writing, but they wouldn't put the agreement in writing. Sure

---

[51] Our boys volunteered to do work similar to the work that the girls, as Candy Stripers, did. The girls worked Saturdays, the boys, Sundays.

enough, when it came time to graduate, he was told he had to stay in the Army for five years. When he told me what happened, I suggested he see the Surgeon General in Washington. When he went, the Surgeon General asked what proof he had of the commitment. Lenny said there were three people who could attest to his plans – the Congressman who recommended him, his Rabbi, and his Scout Master. The Surgeon General told Lenny to get an affidavit from all three of us, then he would see what he could do. Lenny got the affidavits from the three of us, brought them to Washington and got a letter from the Surgeon General that he could go to medical school. Lenny went to Baylor Medical School and graduated. While there, he met a young man who encouraged Lenny to do his residency at an Army hospital. That way, he could do his residency and fulfill his obligation to the Army at the same time. This is what he did in Aurora, Colorado, at the Fitzsimons Army Medical Center, and when he finished he went to a hospital in Texas. About five or six years ago, Lenny delivered octuplets at the Texas Hospital and was on TV[52].

The two Mazzagetti boys went to Rutgers, Dominick on a scholarship. Danny graduated as an accountant, then went into the business field. Dominick was the president of a bank and is also working in the business field. Another young man, Steve Blake, went to college and ended up as a controller for a very large company. Tommy Magsin became a dentist, and Steve

---

[52] A 27-year-old Nigerian-born American woman, Nkem Chukwu, became the mother of the first American-born live set of octuplets, giving birth to six girls and two boys in December, 1998, at St. Luke's Episcopal Hospital in Houston, Texas. One of the girls was born two weeks prior to the others, and all were premature. The smallest girl died a week after birth, but the other seven are thriving today. Mrs. Chukwu was confined to a hospital bed for three months prior to delivery. During the last several weeks, she slept in a near upside-down position to keep pressure off her lower body, and she was on an intravenous diet to make room for the babies. . One of the three delivering doctors was Leonard Weisman, chief neonatal specialist at Texas Children's Hospital.

Putman became a professor at the University of Pennsylvania and is now retired.

Recently, I had a telephone call from David Houseman, who was in my scout troop and now lives in Israel. He went into service in Korea during the '60s and served in the Military Police. When he came home, he decided to go to Israel to visit somebody. While there he met a young lady, and they got married, and he eventually had three children. At first, he was in the Israeli Army as an officer for the MPs. Then he went to college, graduating from Beersheva University, getting a degree in chemistry, and he became a chemist for one of the large companies. Recently, he was reminiscing and wondered what happened to Bernie, so he went on the Internet and when he searched for the name Verosub, he found Ken. He contacted Ken, and Ken told him where I was and gave him my address and telephone number. David called me, then wrote me a lengthy letter, telling me what good memories he had of our time together.

In 1968, I stopped being active as a Scout Master. When I first started, the boys were in patrols. When we would go camping or on trips, each patrol had to provide transportation. The patrol had about eight kids, and there was always someone willing to drive. Around 1967, I was leading a trip to camp and needed transportation for the boys. Nine of the parents sent me $20 to rent a bus, and I said no. When we would go camping, I would get requests asking if a younger son could go with us. I always said yes, as long as the parent would come along. This time, the parents said they didn't want to come – they thought if the younger child went with me, they could take the weekend off. With this kind of attitude, this wasn't the place for me. I had certain ethics. I left the troops after 16 years, ending in 1968. I later became further disenchanted with the Boy Scouts and stopped being a supporter (financially, on their Board, and in arranging for Rabbis to go to the camps on weekends) because they refused to allow a young man who was gay to be a Scout leader. I thought that was terrible. Over the 18 years, I came in contact with an awful lot of boys.

One of my hobbies was saving stamps. I don't know how it started, but I had a very fine collection of stamps, singles of every issue that came out from 1928 on. In the early years, I only saved cancelled stamps. I would ask everyone to save their envelopes for me. Later on, after I had the Post Office in my store, I got my stamps right from the Post Office since the stamps are worth more if they're not cancelled. My printed stamp albums showed me which stamps by year that I needed. One of my most unusual stamps was an issue, I don't recall which one or when, where the stamps were upside down. Right away, I realized these were special and I bought the whole sheet and put them away, and they're very valuable. Ken now has my collection.

Vera and I had decided to spend more time with the kids and not travel so much. In August of 1979, we went to the Poconos and rented a very large house for two weeks where our son, daughter-in-law and children came from California and our daughter, son-in-law and children came from New Jersey. We went swimming and sightseeing, and it was a wonderful two weeks. One afternoon, the four grandchildren (ages 3, 4, 7 and 9) were in the basement, and Vera and I weren't allowed down. The children kept coming up and asking us to cut grapes in half. After dinner that evening, the adults were invited down to the basement, and there was this beautiful layer cake that the grandchildren had baked and decorated with the grapes that we had cut up. We played pin-the-tail on the donkey and other games, and it was a wonderful evening.

Around December 20th of that year, I suddenly had chest pains that woke me at 2:00 in the morning. I thought I was having a heart attack and told Vera she should call 911, then our doctor. We went to St. Barnabas Hospital, where the doctor met us and confirmed that I was having a heart attack. I stayed in the hospital for three weeks. This was difficult because it was Christmas time, and our business was busy. There was no treatment for a heart attack then – just physical therapy and exercises, first in the hospital and then at home. No operation. Very fortunately, I've never had another heart attack, although around 1998, I was given a pacemaker and a defibrillator.

When I went home, I wasn't allowed to go to the store for another 5 weeks, so I looked for projects. I took all our photographs and made a huge frame and a montage of both families.

One of my remembrances of this time was that each time someone came into the store and paid with a silver dollar, I would give it to Vera to put away. At the time of my heart attack, silver dollars had increased in value to about $100 each. We had 800 of them. I was in the hospital at the time, but was in no condition to think of silver dollars, and no one else knew about my plan. So we never cashed them in. Then the value went all the way down to about $7-8 each[53].

While my daughter and the children were staying in our house in Maplewood at this time, their home in Denville was robbed on New Year's Eve. Fortunately, I had insisted that they photograph all their valuables so they had pictures of the dining room table set with their sterling silver and all her jewelry. They had bona fide evidence of what they owned so were able to collect an enormous amount of money from the insurance company.

After I returned to the store, we were robbed in October, 1981. The bandits came down through the roof into the store and turned our postal safe upside down, bashing in the bottom, which was concrete, with my sledge hammer and removing all of the stamps. There were close to 8,000 normal postage stamps plus all the other denominations plus 500 blank money orders which were worth up to $500 each. The inspectors came in and checked everything, and we were absolved of responsibility.

Shortly afterward, Vera and I decided to close the store and sell it. We knew that the Korean community had a society that helped people go into business, and so we advertised in the Korean newspaper in New York and got about 20 responses from people who came out to look at the store. We wanted 100% cash

---

[53] The first silver dollar coin in America was the Spanish eight real piece (known as a Piece of Eight) and was the most common coin in circulation among the thirteen colonies prior to, and even after, independence. It was accepted at the value of one dollar and was irregular in shape, due to their crude method of manufacture. More important was their weight and the purity of the metal. In 1794, the newly organized Philadelphia US Mint began production of the first official US silver dollar coin. However, the Spanish coin and its Mexican successors remained legal tender in the United States until 1857. Today, silver dollar values are determined by age, mint marks denoting the different branch mints, and condition of the coins, known as grading.

and didn't want to take Notes, but none of these people could finance the purchase of the store, so on December 1st, we decided to liquidate. We had big signs saying, "Retiring from Business. Everything in the Store 50% off." By February 1, 1982, we had liquidated the inventory down to $2,000. Someone came in who wanted to buy the business, but we told him we couldn't sell the business since it wasn't viable anymore, but we would sell him the fixtures, air conditioning, gates, etc., and they would have to negotiate with the landlord for the lease. They didn't know it, but we were the landlords. We didn't negotiate with the buyer, but had our attorney do it. We sold the contents of the store for $7,000 and gave the buyer the balance of the stock, valued at $2,000. That was the end of our business as the Mount Vernon Variety Store.

After we sold the store, we found ourselves very much at a loss. We were bored. After 35 years of getting up in the morning and going to work, it was a sudden and rude experience to get up and just be there. I decided to look for a job. Having been a Hallmark greeting card store for all these years, I called Hallmark, and they were very happy to hire me as a merchandiser. I would set up stores that were being opened, setting the stock into the greeting card fixtures, etc. Hallmark also had a lesser line called the Ambassador cards that were in supermarkets and big 5 & 10s and taken care of by their people. I was given 6 Shop Rite markets, and I would go there once a week, straighten out the racks, fill in where cards were missing, put out the holiday cards, remove the holiday cards, etc. I was working there about 6 or 7 months when I was asked to set up a greeting card store. While I was there, the salesman for that store came in and started to tell me what to do. Having been a Hallmark store for 35 years, I knew what they wanted and responded that this was not the Hallmark merchandising method. He wanted me to do it his way, so I told him *he* could do it his way, and I walked out, quitting my job.

Next, I went to a fabric and sewing store that had a picture framing department. They were delighted to see me and I was hired immediately to frame pictures three days a week in the store. When summer came, our son-in-law, Jerry, told Vera and me about a New Jersey Y camp in Milford, Pennsylvania, that needed someone to run their canteen. When we went to see the director of the camp, the director asked what we did, and I told him we had a 5 & 10. We were hired immediately, thanks in much part to Jerry's help. We went in the middle of June to set the canteen up. Although it was an existing canteen, it had never really been run properly. We took care of the campers at the canteen twice a week, during the day. There were 1,000 campers, and they all called us Grandma and Grandpa. In the evenings, we showed a movie and served refreshments to the international staff. College tuition was climbing and camp salaries were not that high, so American students couldn't afford to take jobs in camp. There were two companies in Europe that solicited people to come to America and to work in camps. Since the camps finished by Labor Day and the colleges in Europe didn't start until October, the counselors had the month of September to travel in America, and we often helped plan their vacations. We lived at the camp for the summer, had a lovely room with a private bathroom, and ate in the dining room. The kids would go home about 10 days before Labor Day, then we would stay and close the camp and relax. We got to know young people from all over the world, and it was a lot of fun.

After about 10 years, the director retired, and a new director came in. There was no problem for the first 5 years with the new director, as he made gradual changes. Then one evening, he came into our store and told us that he wanted us to bring in clothing next year – tee shirts, sweat shirts, slacks, shorts -- and sell them in the canteen. Vera and I told him we didn't see the advantage or need since almost everyone brought their own clothes to camp. We didn't want the headache of looking for merchandise, taking care of it, and packing it up at the end of the season for next year. So, after 15 years, we left.

During this time, we volunteered with a number of organizations, although we would take off for the summer when we worked at the camp. We started volunteering in 1982, first at the Newark Museum. I read an article in *New Jersey Magazine* about the museum needing people, so I went there and they were delighted to see me. Of course, the first question always was, "What did you do?" When I told them I had a retail store, the second thing they said was, "You have to meet the manager of our gift shop." I became the buyer of children's toys for the gift shop. Vera volunteered in a different area of the museum, working with the mail and with new member enrollment. At Christmas time, we would load up our station wagon with a variety of gift items and go to the headquarters of various companies, like Hoffman LaRoche, Merck and Kraft Foods. The company would give us a few tables, and we would set up our Christmas display. We were very careful to pick items like jewelry, museum books, diaries, date books, and scarves, and they went over very well. We would sell $1,000 - $1,500 of merchandise each time, never less. We had a plaque given to us for 25 years of service at the museum.[54]

Then I read an article in the *Jewish News* that the Daughters of Israel Geriatric Home was looking for volunteers. Right away, "What did you do? Oh, you have to look at our gift shop." So we took over the gift shop and, once a month on a Sunday, we would go to the East Side in New York to buy for the gift shop – dresses, underwear, all kinds of things. We found a candy company that sold 25-pound boxes of candy that we would buy and split up into 1 pound containers. Periodically, I would write to companies for donations, in all different forms. For example, the houseware stores would send us discontinued items and we would run a garage sale in the lobby of the home. We introduced items in the gift shop that weren't previously available. According to state law, the residents were entitled to commodities likes toothpaste, mouthwash, soap, etc. The home gave it to them, but used generic products. 70 to 80-year-olds don't know about generic products. They only know labels. Colgate, Crest, Scope, and so forth. We brought in the name brand items, and the residents bought from us because they knew the items. We added toys to the shop so the residents could buy a

---

[54]Two of the people I worked with at the Newark Museum came to visit me in July, 2011. Lorelei is the Director and Manager of the gift shop where I worked as a volunteer, and Isabel works in the membership department where Vera used to volunteer. Lorelei begged me to come back to the museum. Since I left, she hasn't been able to find anyone to buy toys for the children's shop. The museum gets 300 to 400 children a day from New Jersey schools, and they stand in line waving $20 bills, waiting to buy something.

toy for when their grandchildren visited. We volunteered there 25 years and our store was very successful.

We also volunteered at the Retired Senior Volunteer Program -- RSVP. In very short order, I became a member of the executive board, and we had a thrift shop in Montclair for used furniture and whatever. We worked there one day a week, for a long time.

The other area where I alone volunteered was income tax preparation. I read an article about AARP's program of preparing income taxes for senior citizens and lower income people. Having always done my own taxes in my business, I had no problem with that. I found out where the work was done, met with the people in charge, and in a short time I was doing income taxes. After about 5 years or so, the man who was the coordinator for the Essex County program retired, so I became the coordinator. I taught and ran the program until 2005.

While all the other volunteer work I did was gratifying, especially the work at the Daughters of Israel because I was really working with people who needed things, the tax program was very, very gratifying work. The cases were really unbelievable. I discovered that many women did not know anything about their finances. Their husband came home, gave them a weekly allowance, and they did what they had to with that, and the husband paid all the bills. I was even more surprised to find that men were no better. They came home, gave their wife their paycheck, she took care of the bills, and he was given $5 for beer money. And he was happy.

There were many many sad cases. For example, a woman came in, telling me she had 5 children. Immediately, I noticed that the family name of the children was different from her last name. When I asked why, she said they were the children of her sister who had died a year and 3 months ago. She said it was very difficult making ends meet because her income was only about $28,000/year. Not much to support 5 children. I asked her, "What about the $18,000 for the children from Social Security? A child of a deceased person gets a little over $300/month until they're 18. 5 kids should get $1,500 a month, times 12 months, or $18,000 a year." Nobody ever told her that. I called a person that I dealt with all the time at the Social Security office and asked her to please give this woman an appointment and make sure to be on time because the woman works by the hour and would lose money. As the woman was leaving, I told her to make sure she got the money retroactive. She didn't know what retroactive meant, so I decided to meet her at her appointment to make sure she got everything she deserved. She ended up getting an additional $18,000 a year, which was significant to her, plus the retroactive money. There were many cases similar to this, but this was the most gratifying because there was a lot of money involved.

I was also an arbitrator for the NJ Supreme Court. The Supreme Court is very interesting work. The object is to reduce the need for court cases in lawsuits between attorneys and their clients, mostly over the fees. Depending on the county, they have committees of two attorneys and one lay person. Once a month, you go to the court house and listen to the client and the attorney present their case, usually three or four cases at a time. Then the three-man committee comes to a decision which is binding, and the involved parties have to abide by the decision. It's very interesting to hear some of the fees that the attorneys get, and also very interesting to hear their explanations supporting their fees. You do it for four years, then take off a year, then do it for four more. I did it three times. I got a service plaque for this too.

We sold the Maplewood house in 1995. It took us a year to dispose of the extra stuff that we had, and we moved to a magnificent apartment in Morris Plains, Powder Mill Heights, the new ones on the hill. We became friendly with a number of people in the complex. There was a promenade, and we used to go down every evening and walk it in good weather. One day, a couple we had become friendly with said they were moving to Fox Hills, a condominium complex with 14 buildings and 42 apartments in most buildings. We looked at the condominium, liked it very much, and bought one in 1998. It took until the end of 2000 for the building that we were going into to be finished. We moved in February of 2001 and were very happy there until 2008. We met two couples, our neighbors across the hall, Cynthia (Cindy) and Sanford (Sandy) Chase, and Seena and Ira Solomon, who lived in the Madison building, with whom we became particularly good friends. We frequently would go to the movies, to dinner and to many functions together.

Vera always had various health problems, but nothing major until the last couple of years when her health began deteriorating significantly. In January, 2008, she had trouble breathing, and the doctor gave her some medication and exercises. We had to make a difficult decision. Vera was not feeling well, but our grandson, Douglas, was getting married to Jessica in Washington, DC, and we both were to be part of the bridal party. The decision was made to go. We went via our son-in-law's car and stayed at a large hotel near the Capitol. Jessica's family, Kenneth and Carol Adelman, are both very much involved in politics and have had various government positions from time to time, so this was to be a very large wedding with lots of people. We went down on Thursday because there were festivities on Friday and luncheons on Saturday, one for the women of the bride and groom families and one for the men. The wedding in the evening was elaborate. Vera and I led the procession, followed by a number of little ones who were nieces and nephews of the bride and groom, followed by bridesmaids and ushers. It was a lovely affair and we had a wonderful evening, returning on Sunday to New Jersey.

Vera managed to get through the weekend, but around February 5th she didn't feel well, so we went to the emergency room at St. Clare's Hospital. They took some x-rays and tests, then put her in the hospital. She had something wrong with her lungs. A little part of the lung controls breathing and the use of oxygen, and this wasn't functioning properly. She kept going down and down, and then around the 18th of February, we transferred her to hospice in Dover and she passed away on Friday, the 22nd. Fortunately, she did not suffer a long time. We did everything together over our 67 years together. We went to work together in the store, we volunteered together. Occasionally she would play mahjongg or canasta with her ladies, but basically we were always together.

I periodically visit the Veterans Administration Hospital in order to be eligible for medications and other things. In September, 2008, I was making my usual visitation. Following the visit I always socialized with the nurse-practitioner, Carla Francis, with whom I have become very good friends. As we were talking, she detected a bump on my neck which I hadn't noticed and immediately sent me for a CAT scan and x-ray.

Finding a tumor in my thyroid gland, the recommendation was for me to see a specialist/surgeon at a hospital in Newark. He operated and then I went to Dr. Bari, an oncologist, who recommended radiation therapy. Wearing a large plastic mask, I received the radiation treatments at the Dover branch of St. Clare's Hospital, five days a week for seven weeks. The people in the Fox Hills building where I lived were wonderful and provided me with transportation to and from the hospital every day of those seven weeks. Following the treatment, I was told to take certain medications and to take things easy, however the treatments had an effect on my throat, cutting down the space to a point where it was difficult to swallow. A tube was inserted in my stomach and three times a day, for over a year, I would receive nutrients and medications through the tube. After a while, it was determined that I should go to Merry Heart in Boonton Township for rehab to help build up my endurance. I had to learn how to walk again, and I was there for 23 days. I still have trouble swallowing, but no longer have the tube. I'm able to eat, but I carefully cut my food up so that the pieces are small, and I chew very carefully.

 I stayed in the apartment until 2009, when I moved here to Victoria Mews. I had a huge apartment at Fox Hills, two big bedrooms, a living room/dining room that was huge, double the size of my room now, a sun parlor, two bathrooms, a kitchen and a balcony. At this point, I was a little shaky and walking with a walker. Everybody kept telling me that I wasn't going to be able to manage, and my son and daughter were not happy with my continuing to drive. I was alone and had to do my own cooking, so we decided to hire some help from Grannies Nannies for three hours at a time. Someone would take me shopping and would prepare the evening meal and I had another woman who came in once a week to clean, but I still had to do laundry and some other household tasks, and it didn't work out. So we looked into assisted living and checked out several of them. We didn't find most acceptable, but Victoria Mews was. I moved in here June 1, 2009, and this June (2011) will be two years. One of the first things that impressed me was that when we walked in the door, everyone said hello. When we went to Sunrise in Randolph and in Morris Plains, it was like going into an icebox. Nobody talked, but here everyone says hello, good morning, how are you. I also liked that they came in every morning to make my bed and remove the trash, I get three meals a day, and my laundry is done each week. Any time of the day, if I want a cup of coffee or juice, there is a Bistro downstairs where I can help myself. There are activities, but they're not for me. They're geared more for the women, but I manage to find activities. I created my own. I created a library of hardback books and a library of paperback books, complete with inventory. I set up and operate a store. I run activities, like slide shows of my trips and a horse race game. I find things to do, like organize another resident's pictures into a montage for her.

I have one more goal – to be here for the wedding of my first great grandchild, Sarah. She's 13. In the meantime, I'll keep busy.

l to r: Aaron Verozub, Vladimir Verozub, and Reuben Verozub, author's grandfather (Kiev, Ukraine, circa 1910)

Misha Golostupitz (Golos); Kolia Verozub (Verosub), author's father (Kiev, Ukraine, circa 1910)

My Life 77

3rd from l: Kolia Verosub   2nd from r: Misha Golos
(Kiev, Ukraine, circa 1910)

l to r: Kolia & Anuta Verosub, author's parents; Hyman Goloub, Octave Golos (New York City, 1923)

1st row, l to r: Leo Verosub, Rubia Verosub, author's sister, Anuta Verosub, Bernard Verosub, Fannie Golos;
2nd row, l to r: Kolia Verozub, Octave Golos, Misha Golos
(New York City, 1927)

Anuta Verosub (l), author's mother
(Napanoch, NY, 1928)

*Fannie & Misha Golos
(New York City, 1919)*

*Rubia Verosub &
Lucian Kaminsky
(Bronx, NY, 1928)*

*Vera and Bernard Verosub, wedding day,
Sept. 21, 1942, New York City*

Senior Lifebook project needs volunteers
Wednesday, March 23, 2011
BY DONNA ROLANDO
SUBURBAN TRENDS
STAFF WRITER

June Moffa of Butler says her children's grandfather died before she could fulfill her desire to write his story for future generations.

STAFF PHOTO BY JOE SARNO

Volunteer Sharon Palmer of Boonton helps 91-year-old Bernard Verosub write the story of his life.

But because of her efforts as a volunteer for Lifebook Writing Project, which is telling senior citizens' life stories in Morris and now Passaic counties, other families will have their memories preserved.

"I absolutely ended up loving it," said Moffa of her experience working with Edna Herziger, a 99-year-old Montville senior who was eager to get the writing process started.

"She had quite a history to share of things that she lived through," said Moffa, like how she would picnic with her family on the Hudson watching the George Washington Bridge under construction.

A survivor of The Great Depression, she also made her own clothes from scrap and became quite sufficient as a dressmaker, Moffa recalled.

Although Moffa was the volunteer, she said, "I ended up getting more than I feel that I gave."

Her experience writing Herziger's Lifebook, through an ongoing project of Skylands RSVP & Volunteer Resource Center, in connection with Northwest NJ Community Action Program Inc. (NORWESCAP), brought her the gift of friendship with this golden-ager.

Ellen Konwiser, special projects coordinator for NORWESCAP, came up with the idea of the Lifebook Writing Project, which began three years ago in Morris County and is now branching into Passaic County starting with West Milford. Though the agency has 25 active volunteers at 12 senior community sites, there is always the need for more – those able to capture these stories on a voice recorder and type them up on a computer. The end result is put into a binder for families to treasure.

What she has learned through these years of listening is that "nobody's life is boring," Konwiser said. "Some of the people have had the most amazing lives."

Bernard Verosub, who lives at Victoria Mews assisted living in Township of Boonton, is one of those eye-openers. At 91 years, his life spans from World War II service making maps of Japan (based on his photos with the 41st air reconnaissance squadron), to a career as a novelty store owner and inventor.

Back in the day, younger children had him to thank for a hula hoop that was just their size. For Verosub, then co-owner of L & B Novelty Company, it was the perfect solution for 60,000 pieces of quarter-inch plastic tubing he no longer had use for.

Bernard Verosub

The last of a generation, Verosub saw his story as important enough to family history to take up the task of writing it all down himself, but found himself stalled.

That's why he embraced the Lifebook Writing Project and working with volunteer Sharon Palmer of Boonton.

"He was always an opportunist but in a really good way. He developed all kinds of new products," said Palmer, like the Happy Birdie parakeet that graced many pet owners' cages and was on the market for roughly 10 years.

Being an inventor went along well with his work at Mount Vernon Variety Store in Newark, which he ran with Vera, his wife of 65 years who died in February 2008.

When a break-in left their store in a shambles, they decided to retire in the early 1980s.

"We didn't want to be carried out; we wanted to walk out," he said.

Closing one door and opening another, Verosub volunteered for 25 years in the gift shop at the Newark Museum serving as "buyer of toys" and followed that up with 17 years as a volunteer – again in a gift shop for Daughters of Israel. He and Vera worked with children during the summer at the Y camp in Pennsylvania – for 17 years running the canteen. He was also volunteered as an arbitrator for the NJ Supreme Court for 12 years and as an AARP tax preparer for many years.

When Verosub's book is done, it will be presented to his family, but one day Konwiser hopes to also be able to share stories, such as these, in some form with the rest of northern New Jersey.

If these stories have drawn your interest, perhaps you might have what it takes to be a volunteer. All volunteers receive free training in the Lifebook process. For more information call Konwiser at 973-784-4900 ext. 103. E-mail: rolando@northjersey.com

Sunday, April 20, 2008   THE SUNDAY STAR-LEDGER

A master of trivia and volunteering

BERNARD VEROSUB
88, Rockaway Township

By Nancy Degutis

Accomplishment

A volunteer for various organizations for 55 years and now the "Trivia Master" of Fox Hills Condominiums.

When Verosub walked into a Cub Scout Pack 104 meeting in 1952, he came to enroll his son, but the New York City native came out of the meeting as the leader,

In the half-century since, he has volunteered for several groups, carrying on a family creed he inherited and uses today with the gusto of a person half his age.

"My dad and uncle were immigrants who helped others like them left and right because people had helped them become established. My father brought a man, his wife, two children (from the Soviet Union) home in 1925. They lived with us for six months," recalled Verosub, who has passed that legacy on to his children and grandchildren, who also are involved in volunteering.

Doing business six days a week

A graduate of New York University, Verosub earned his bachelor of science degree in aeronautical engineering in 1942, the year he married Vera, his wife of 65 years. After World War II, they considered opening a chicken farm but opted instead to go into retailing.

The couple owned and ran a 2,000-square-foot retail variety store in the Ivy Hill section of Newark. After their marriage in 1942, they worked "side-by-side, always," opening the business at 7 a.m. and closing at 6 p.m. six days a week for 35 years.

They retired in 1982, but when their son-in-law became director of a YMWHA youth camp in the Poconos, he suggested they run the canteen there. For 13 years "we had 1,000 grandchildren every summer. To us, it was really a vacation."

Changes in life

After Verosub read an article in a New Jersey magazine about how the Newark Museum needed volunteers, he interviewed with museum officials and used his retailing experience to buy items for the gift shop.

He did the same type pf work during the 25 years he was at the Daughters of Israel Geriatric Center in West Orange, later running a men's woodworking program there. His wife joined in, offering her services at the center.

Verosub also joined the AARP Tax Aide Program and became the program's Essex County coordinator. He also offered his services as an arbitrator/mediator to the Morris County Court System for eight years and the Rockaway Township Court System for five years. He also worked in the Rockaway Township school system for five years.

Master of trivia

Verosub's latest venture is "Trivia with Bernie" nights at Fox Hills at Rockaway, an active adult community where the couple now lives. The monthly Thursday evening sessions draw 40 to 50 residents who make up two teams.

"I buy two Megabucks lottery tickets for the team that wins and who split (lottery) money they could win with me. So far, the most we have gotten is $7," he quipped.

Proudest accomplishment

The couple raised two children, Kenneth, a son who is a geophysics professor at University of California Davis, and their daughter, Eileen Sackin, a Denville resident who heads a private nursery school. The Verosubs also have four grandchildren and three great-grandchildren.

Sunday, October 21, 2007   THE DAILY RECORD

Mr. and Mrs. Bernard Verosub

Vera and Bernard B. Verosub celebrated their 65th anniversary at two events—a Labor Day weekend celebration with their family and a reception in their honor at Fox Hills in Rockaway. They were married Sept. 21, 1942, in New York City. Formerly of Maplewood and Morris Plains, they now reside in Rockaway. The couple retired in 1982 after 35 years as owners of the Mount Vernon Variety Store in Newark. Since retirement, both have volunteered at the Daughters of Israel Geriatric Center, the Newark Museum, and the Retired and Senior Volunteer Program in Essex County. Mr. Verosub is an arbitrator for the Ethics Committee of the New Jersey court system in Morris County and has served as a mediator in Rockaway Township. After serving for 25 years in the American Association of Retired Persons Tax Aide Program, he retired this year after 15 years. The couple's children and their respective spouses are—a son, Kenneth Verosub, and his wife, Irina, of Davis, Calif., and a daughter, Eileen, and her husband, Gerald Sackin, of Denville. The couple also have four grandchildren and three great-grandchildren.

December 23, 2004   NJJN — METRO WEST

For 85-year-old volunteer, idleness 'is for old people'

By Robert Wiener
NJJN Staff Writer

Bernard Verosub retired in 1982 as owner and operator of the Mount Vernon Variety Store in the Ivy Hill section of Newark, but that doesn't mean he's slowing down.

At the age of 85 he scoffs at the notion.

"Nah," he said. "That's for old people."

What keeps him busy is a wide variety of services he performs as a volunteer—enterprises that earned him the 2004 Andrus Award for Community Service from AARP, the American Association of Retired Persons. The award was presented to Verosub at a Dec. 13 program in Princeton.

In a statement, the AARP congratulated Verosub on "his remarkable efforts to make a difference in the lives of others."

Verosub's first effort was at the Newark Museum, where he worked in the gift shop.

Then, he joined Tax Aide, a collaboration between AARP and the Internal Revenue Service, which aids hundreds of needy people in preparing their tax returns.

"All the years I was in business I did my own taxes, so I figured I could help others," he said. Sometimes his assistance to others has paid off—in dollars for his clients and satisfaction for himself.

"I had a teenage mother with a two-and-a-half-year-old child, who earned $10,000 a year from two part-time jobs while her mother took care of the kid. I helped her get a $2,500 refund on her taxes."

He informed another client—the guardian of her late sister's five children—that they were entitled to monthly Social Security checks. "I told her what documents she needed when she applied for 18 months of retroactive payments." Then I explained what 'retroactve' meant. Her family is now collecting $18,000 a year."

In between tax seasons, Verosub keeps busy running a sheltered workshop for residents of the Daughters of Israel Nursing Home in West Orange. The chores the people do may be routine—putting combs in plastic containers and then boxing them to be shipped—but no one is complaining.

"It beats having them sit around all day like zombies," he said. "The workshop opens at 10 in the morning, and by 9:15 they are waiting outside in the hall, eager to get to work."

When he isn't on duty at the nursing home, Verosub serves as a volunteer arbitrator with the Morris County court system, helping to resolve disputes that arise when attorneys and their clients argue over fees, a task he considers challenging.

He and his wife, Vera, live in the Fox Hills development in Rockaway, where he enjoys playing still another volunteer role—that of quizmaster. When residents get together for trivia contests, "I make up the questions, and I give the winners Megabucks lottery tickets. So I could be giving someone $25 million."

Verosub said the impulse to volunteer is practically a part of his DNA.

"It came from my father and my uncle," he said, "and I tell my children and grandchildren [the Verosubs have a son, a daughter, four grandchildren, and three great grandchildren] that they must help other people. The gratification they get is far greater than the effort they put in."

Despite that imperative, and the busy schedule it imposes on his own life, he carves out time for relaxation.

"We used to travel all over the United States," he said.

But as he observes the 25th anniversary "of my one and only heart attack," he and his wife enjoy staying close to home—where he insists there is plenty to do.

"We go to lectures. We have subscriptions at the Paper Mill Playhouse and NJPAC. We are going to the film festivals at Morris County College and the JCC."

But the Verosubs are not going to Florida.

"That's where the old folks go."

Saturday, October 23, 2004   DAILY RECORD

SENIOR PROFILE

Rockaway man earns AARP volunteer award

85-year-old pitches in wherever he is needed

By Jillian Riseberg
SPECIAL TO THE DAILY RECORD

To give of oneself is the act of taking the "I" out of the equation and making it about the "you."

Bernard Verosub, 85, of Rockaway, has spent more than two decades helping make life easier for senior citizens.

He started long before it was fashionable to be a volunteer.

In recognition of his commitment to volunteerism, AARP New Jersey has chosen Verosub as the 2004 recipient of its Andrus Award for Community Service for New Jersey.

AARP's most prestigious volunteer award will be presented to Verosub at a luncheon next month in Princeton.

Verosub said he was "free and going mad" after retiring in 1982 as owner of the Mount Vernon Variety Store in Newark.

Then, he saw a magazine article about the Newark Museum needing volunteers.

For 20 years, he worked in the museum's gift shop and later did most of the buying of toys and novelties for children.

"At that time, when I came to volunteer at the museum, there were about 69 volunteers—68 women and me," he said. "Now there are 189. It has become quite popular to volunteer, you might say."

Verosub then responded to an ad requesting volunteers at Daughters of Israel in West Orange. "There I was running a woodworking program for men," he said.

For 22 years, he also managed the gift shop there, doubling as a buyer and volunteer recruiter.

Help with taxes

Verosub also started volunteering with the AARP Tax Aide program.

"During the years I was in business, I never had an accountant," he said. "I did all my tax returns myself and everything business-wise was done by me."

When an Essex County coordinator retired, he told Verosub: "You should take over because you know what we're doing and how we do it."

"Depending on the year, I've had as little as 50 and as many as 60 people working on the tax program," he said.

Tirza Freeman, a former accountant who has worked with Verosub in the AARP Tax Aide program nominated him for the Andrus Award.

She said Verosub handles federal and state tax matters.

"He assembles all these materials and I can tell you it involves a tremendous amount of patience because there are thousands of documents," she said.

Freeman said that while many people Verosub's age are sitting around talking about getting old, he does the opposite.

"He does no such thing," she said. "He's a real role model for me because he's always upbeat, he wants to help people, he wants to improve people.

"He feels that you should spend your time in helping others, not in being sorry for yourself, and that's a good thing."

Freeman said Verosub doesn't dwell on his problems; instead he concentrates on what he can do next.

"I just feel that he is making the most out of his life and he does it with good will and good humor," she said. "I think he's a great guy."

Currently, Verosub is a fee arbitrator with the ethics committee of the New Jersey court system in Morris County.

Five committees made up of two lawyers and a layperson try to settle claims between clients and lawyers.

"Our decisions are binding," said Verosub, who also serves as a mediator with the Rockaway Township Municipal Court.

'He gets younger'

The Retired and Senior Volunteer Program, Daughters of Israel, the Newark Museum, and the Greater Volunteer Council of Essex County have honored Verosub and his wife, Vera, for outstanding volunteer service.

Lynn Hendershot, who directs the work activity center at Daughters of Israel, said: "He's well-known for always doing a great job at whatever he's volunteering at in the nursing home. He has a lot of patience, and the residents love him.

"He takes it on his own initiative to help other people; he really is a take-charge kind of person and very sharp."

Hendershot has known Verosub for years in and out of the center's setting, and she said he is a devoted husband and father, very energetic, systematic and organized.

"It's so great to know you can rely on him, and even personally, he's been very understanding," she said. "He gets younger instead of older. He's just really a great guy, and I'm so glad he's getting this award."

Veteran of WWII

When their son-in-law took a job as director of the New Jersey Y Camps in the Poconos, he told Verosub that the camp was looking for someone to run the canteen.

"So for 13 summers, we had a thousand grandchildren," Verosub said.

A Bronx native, Verosub is a 1937 alumnus of DeWitt Clinton High School.

He is a 1942 graduate of New York University with a bachelor of science degree in aeronautical engineering.

Verosub said he would have graduated sooner, but while pursuing his studies, the Army Signal Corps assigned him to training classes at Swarthmore College. It was nearly a year before he returned.

As a private first class in the Army Air Forces during World War II, Verosub was stationed in Guam in a photo-reconnaissance squadron, a mission that he later realized had historic significance.

"I participated—at the time I didn't know that I was making them for that purpose—but I participated in making target maps for Nagasaki and Hiroshima," he said.

When his service ended in 1946, Verosub and his wife were going to settle on a chicken farm.

"But we didn't find one to my uncle's liking because he thought everything was too expensive," he said.

The couple lived in Hillside for five years in Newark, where Vera was born and raised.

Trying his hand at retail, Verosub opened a hardware, housewares, paint and garden supply store in Newark because four-family homes were being built in the area.

"The homes weren't selling, so they were building two-family houses, then built the Ivy Hill Apartments, which are five buildings with 500 families in each building," he said. "We figured that this should be a good business and there wasn't any (store) in that location."

But after the larger buildings were constructed, the Verosubs didn't see the need for garden supplies and paints.

Verosub said, "We converted it into a 5-and-10 and general store, besides all the usual things of greeting cards, fabrics, knitting wool, needlepoint, school supplies—whatever you want we had—we also were a contract station for the post office."

While living in Newark, the Verosubs became members of the Beth David Jewish Center.

"I went to meetings to enroll my son as a Cub Scout and walked out as a Cub master," Verosub said, adding that for 18 years, he was both Cub master and scoutmaster of the Boy Scouts at the temple.

In 1957, the Verosubs moved to Maplewood, where they lived until 1995, when they began calling Morris Plains home. From there, they moved to Rockaway.

Their son, Kenneth, is a professor of geology at the University of California at Davis.

Their daughter, Eileen, is a nursery school teacher in private day care at Discovery Years Preschool & Nursing in the Whippany section of Hanover.

Verosub and his wife have two granddaughters, two grandsons, and three great-grandchildren.

The couple met on a blind date in May 1941. They celebrated their 62-year wedding anniversary September 21.

Describing his father and uncle, both immigrants from Kiev, Ukraine, as good teachers, Verosub said he saw how much they cared about others, and he followed their example.

"Their creed was helping other people," he said. "About a year or two after I started doing the various volunteer work, I realized that there's a lot to be done and I can do a lot of good. It's really about helping people in all walks of life."

Made in the USA
San Bernardino, CA
26 October 2014